THE MAD OLD ADS

THE MAD OLD ADS

DICK SUTPHEN

W. H. ALLEN · LONDON · 1968

First British edition, 1968
Printed and bound in Great Britain
by The Garden City Press Ltd,
Letchworth
for the publishers
W. H. ALLEN & COMPANY
Essex Street, London WC2
491 00291 2

SPECIAL THANKS TO SYBIL O'HAGAN AND BOB SUTPHEN
FOR THEIR HELP IN COMPILING THIS BOOK

The material in this volume has been compiled from actual old newspapers, magazines and books. The facts used in the case histories, and many of the earliest ads are from the book "A History of Advertising," published in England in 1874.

Today an individual with constipation, St. Vitus's Dance and the opium habit would have a real problem. But in the 1880's, according to the ads, all he needed was a Health Jolting Chair and Dr. Buckland's Scotch Oats Essence to solve all his problems.

How can a giant in a washing machine for the purpose of selling soap, compare to a Magnetico-Electric Celestial Bed supported by twenty-eight glass pillars for the purpose of creating fertility in childless couples.

A cigarette that tastes good like a cigarette should can hardly parallel one guaranteed to cure all diseases of the throat and foul breath too.

If you believe advertising is getting wilder and more preposterous by the day, the material in this volume will certainly alter your opinion. Present-day advertisers try to outdo each other with attention-getting gimmicks. In the past an advertiser simply used a wilder claim than his competitors whether it was true or not.

We now have motivational research, marketing experts and computers to turn selling into a scientific art. Yet I defy any computer to pinpoint a market more effectively than an Illinois undertaker of the mid-1800's who sent the following letter to sick people:

> "Dear Sir, having positive proof that you are rapidly approaching Death's gate, I have, therefore, thought it not imprudent to call your attention to the enclosed advertisement of my abundant stock of ready-made coffins, and desire to make the suggestion that you signify to your friends a wish for the purchase of your burial outfit at my establishment."

Has advertising advanced or regressed over the years? Has it become more or less exciting? The following collection of the maddest of the mad old ads will help you decide for yourself. Today's ads are certainly more subdued and restrained than their predecessors, and with federal controls they are probably more believable. But I'm sure great-great-grandfather believed the proclamations of his day too.

Contents:

In the Beginning...

Public criers and signs over shops and stalls seem naturally to have been the first efforts in the direction of advertisements, and they go back to the most remote portions of the world's history.

In Pompeii and similar places, advertising by means of signs and inscriptions was quite common. The "History of Signboards," a very exhaustive and valuable book, quotes Aristotle, and refers to Lucian, Aristophanes, and others, in proof of the fact that signboard advertisements were used in ancient Greece. This particular ad was discovered painted on a Pompeii wall:

THERE WILL BE A DEDICATION OR
FORMAL OPENING OF CERTAIN BATHS.
THOSE ATTENDING ARE PROMISED SLAUGHTER
OF WILD BEASTS, ATHLETIC GAMES,
PERFUMED SPRINKLING, AND
AWNINGS TO KEEP OFF THE SUN.

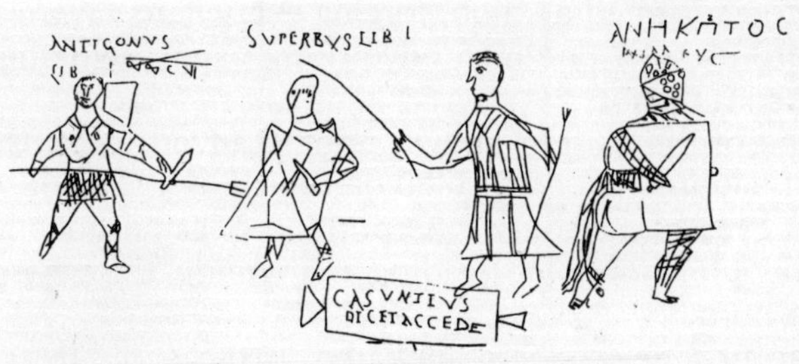

From a wall in Pompeii.
This inscription was promoting a contest of gladiators.

The first graphic symbolism in signs was probably introduced when the various artificers of Rome used their tools as signs over their workshops and residences. A gravedigger used a pickaxe and a lamp, a baker used a bushel measure, a millstone and some ears of corn. This form of advertising gradually grew, until, in the Middle Ages, there was hardly a house of business without its distinctive symbol.

As luxury increased, and the number of houses or shops dealing in the same article multiplied, something more was needed. Since particular trades were confined to particular streets, the next step was to give each shop a name or token by which it might be mentioned in conversation, so that it could be recommended and customers sent to it. During this period few people could read, so to write the owner's name would have been of little use.

Those who could advertised their name with symbols — thus a hare and a bottle stood for Harebottle, and two cocks for Cox. Those whose names could not be represented in this way adopted pictorial objects such as portraits of great men in history.

Some of the early generic symbols are still in use today, such as the barber's pole and the pawn broker's three gilded balls.

As the idea of advertising grew, the ideas themselves became wilder. In 1141, the public criers in France scurried about in the streets crying the merits of a particular tavern. They carried a large wooden measure of wine, from which to offer samples of the product they proclaimed. By 1258 the criers formed a union, forcing every Paris tavern owner to hire its own one-man advertising agency whether they wanted it or not.

One of the earliest known printed advertisements was a small handbill issued in 1480 on behalf of a religious book, "The Pyes of Salisbury." As printing became general, and the people conquered reading and writing, the newspapers were born.

The first newspapers appeared in the early 1600's, and they soon began to carry ads, which were primarily for new books or for lost items.

Numb. 49

Domestick Intelligence,

Or, News both from

CITY and COUNTRY,

Published to prevent false Reports.

Tuesday, *Decemb.* 23. 1679.

Photographed from an actual English newspaper of 1679, this shows the form of most early printed advertisements.

Advertiſements.

THeſe are to give Notice That the Right Honourable the Lord. Maior, *and the Commiſsioners of Serveyors for the City of* London, *and the Liberties thereof; have conſtituted and appointed* Samuel Potts *and* Robert Davies, *Citizens; tob· the General Rakers of the ſaid City and Lib·rties, and do keep their Office in Red Lyon Court, in* Watling-ſtreet, *where any Perſon or Perſons that are deſirous to be Imployed under them, as Carters and Sweepers of the Streets, may repair from Eight a Clock in the morning, till twelve a Clock at noon, and from two till ſix at night, where they may be entertained accordingly: And if any Gardners, Farmers or others will be furniſht with any Dung Soyl or Compaſt, may there agree for it at reaſonable rates; and all Gentlemen having private Stables, and all Inholders and Maſters of Livery Stables and all others, are deſired to repair thither for the carrying away of their Dung and Soil from their reſpective Stables, and other plaes, according to an Act of Common Council for that purpoſe.*

THere is newly publiſbed a Pack of Cards, containing an Hiſtory of all the Popiſh *Plots that have been in* England; *beginning with thoſe in Queen* Elizabeth *time, and ending with this laſt damnable Plot againſt his Majeſty* Charles II: *Excellently engraven on Copper Plates, with very larg deſcriptions under each Card The like not extant. Sold by* Randal Taylor *near* Stationers-hall, *and* Benjamin Harris *at the* Stationers Arms *under the* Royal Exchange *in* Cornhill.

THe Milleners Goods that was to be Sold at the Naked Boy near Strand Bridge, are Sold at Mr. Vanden Anker *in* Limeſtreet.

LOſt on Sunday night the 21 Inſtant in the Meuſe, *a pocket with a Watch in a ſingle Studded Caſe, made by* Richard Lyons; *alſo a Bunch of Keyes, and other things: whoever brings them to Mr.* Bently *in* Covent-Garden, *or Mr.* Allen *at the* Meuſe Gate *ſhall have 20 s, Reward.*

In 1679 a London haberdasher named Jonathan Holder came up with an idea regarded as a dangerous innovation by his peers. To every purchaser spending more than one guinea, he gave a printed list of the articles he stocked and their prices. His competitors felt this would be quite destructive to trade if shopkeepers lavished so much of their capital in printing useless handbills.

In the early 1800's, billstickers were considered a nuisance of the most intolerable kind. They cared nothing for the privacy of open walls, residences, street doors or any surface on which they could paste a poster. Any billsticker worth his salt considered it a point of honor to paste over the work of a rival, and his disfigurative work became a prominent feature of a city.

Out of necessity, advertising contractors were born. They purchased the exclusive rights to stick bills on a particular place. The idea of these contractors began to grow, and they extended their operations to subletting spaces in metropolitan railway stations, and then expanded by placing announcements on the sides of the cars in the form of little enamelled plates.

Imaginative new medias were created, one being the practice of stencilling ads on flagstones on private property. This practice resulted in police action.

As competition grew more fierce, the advertisers became more creative. One of the most interesting approaches to make a lasting impression was developed by an English newspaper in 1855. The paper's name was stamped into every pence and halfpence coin they could obtain. This particular advertising media ended with the interference of Parliament and helped to necessitate a vote of 10,000 pounds to replace all the battered money.

By the mid-1800's, advertising had become big business, and the newspapers and periodicals were collecting big revenues for helping to spread the word. Businessmen were limited only by their imagination and integrity. The quacks and charlatans had a new way to dupe the public in mass. The hucksters had arrived.

Quacks and Imposters

The origin of quackery, for the purpose of making money, is unknown. It is evident that it evolved naturally as civilization advanced. With the advent of printed advertising, the quacks had a way to dupe the public in mass, and they grew and flourished.

In the 1700's and even well into the 1800's, many people believed that the seventh son of a seventh son naturally possessed great medical and healing powers. Some historians believe that quackery in general was caused by this quaint superstition. In many areas of Europe, as late as 1880, the seventh son of a seventh son would automatically be called "doctor."

Naturally many of the early quacks claimed to be seventh sons, which gave them a distinct advantage over their competitors. There is no doubt that with their careless compounding of drugs, they killed more than they cured.

One particular individual was exposed, though it didn't seem to harm him, in an article in the English publication "Gentleman's Magazine" of July, 1734. The paragraph ran:

"There was an extraordinary advertisement in the newspapers this month concerning the great cures in all distempers performed with one medicine, a pill or drop, by Joshua Ward, Esq., lately arrived from Paris, where he had done the like cures. 'Twas said our physicians, particularly Sir Hans Sloane, had found out his secret, but 'twas judged so violent a prescription, that it would be deemed malpractice to apply it as a dose to old and young and in all cases."

The following unfavorable advertisement ran in the same publication about two years later.

> *Vesey Hart*, Esq. of *Lincoln's Inn*. About 15 Months ago he took the celebrated Pill, which had at first such violent effects as to throw him into Convulsions and deprive him of his Sight. On recovery he fell into Consumption.

Joshua Ward was quite a celebrity about this time, even among the quacks. In the "'Daily Advertiser" of June 10, 1736, there is a boasting ad for Ward, which runs:

> We hear that by the Queen's appointment, Joshua Ward, Esq ; and eight or ten persons, who in extraordinary Cases have receiv'd great benefit by taking his remedies, attended at the Court at Kensington on monday night last, and his patients were examin'd before her Majesty by three eminent surgeons, several persons of quality being present, when her Majesty was graciously pleas'd to order money to be distributed amongst the patients, and congratulated Mr Ward on his great success.

The "Grub Street Journal," another local paper, enjoyed exposing quacks. On June 24th of the same year they ran an article which stated that only seven persons attended at the palace, and that these were proved to be imposters who were in collusion with Ward. The article concludes with the following lines.

> *Seven wonderful Cures.*
>
> One felt his sharp rheumatic pains no more :
> A Second saw much better than before :
> Three cur'd of stone, a dire disease much sadder,
> Who still, 'tis thought, have each a stone in bladder :
> A Sixth brought gravel bottled up and cork'd,
> Which *Drop and Pill*, he say'd, by urine work'd ;
> But Questions, ask'd the Patient, all unravell'd ;
> Much more than whom the Doctor then was gravell'd.
> The last a little Woman but great glutton,
> Who at one meal eat two raw legs of mutton :

The earliest quack cure all ad we could find is from a 1664 edition of the English publication "News."

SMALL BAGGS to hang about Children's necks, which are excellent both for the *prevention and cure* of the *Rickets*, and to ease Children in breeding of Teeth, are prepared by Mr Edmund Buckworth, and constantly to be had at Mr Philip Clark's, Keeper of the Library in the Fleet, and nowhere else, at 5 shillings a bagge.

This truly marvelous plan for greasing the tongue ran in the original edition of the English newspaper "Spectator" in 1711.

AN admirable confect which assuredly cures Stuttering and Stammering in children or grown persons, though never so bad, causing them to speak distinct and free without any trouble or difficulty; it remedies all manner of impediments in the speech or disorders of the voice of any kind, proceeding from what cause soever, rendering those persons capable of speaking easily and free, and with a clear voice who before were not able to utter a sentence without hesitation. Its stupendous effects in so quickly and infallibly curing Stammering and all disorders of the voice and difficulty in delivery of the speech are really wonderful. Price 2s. 6d. a pot, with directions. Sold only at Mr Osborn's Toyshop, at the Rose and Crown, under St Dunstan's church Fleet street.

Also from the original edition of the "Spectator."

LOSS of Memory, or Forgetfulness, certainly cured by a grateful electuary peculiarly adapted for that end; it strikes at the primary source, which few apprehend, of forgetfulness, makes the head clear and easy, the spirits free, active, and undisturbed, corroborates and revives all the noble faculties of the soul, such as thought, judgment, apprehension, reason and memory, which last in particular it so strengthens as to render that faculty exceeding quick and good beyond imagination; thereby enabling those whose memory was before almost totally lost, to remember the minutest circumstances of their affairs, etc. to a wonder. Price 2s. 6d. a pot. Sold only at Mr Payne's, at the Angel and Crown, in St Paul's Churchyard, with directions.

In 1700 this appeal from one quack consists of a warning against all others of the same profession. Shown here only partially because of its length, it ends with a sales pitch for his own miraculous healing powers.

A CAUTION TO THE UNWARY.

'Tis generally acknowledged throughout all Europe, that no Nation has been so fortunate in producing such eminent Physicians, as this Kingdom of ours; and 'tis as obvious to every Eye, that no Country was ever pestered with so many ignorant Quacks or Empirics. The Enthusiast in Divinity having no sooner acted his Part, and had his *Exit*, but on the same Stage, from his Shop (or some worse Place) enters the Enthusiast in Physicks: yesterday a Taylor, Heelmaker, Barber, Serving Man, Rope Dancer, etc., to-day *per saltum* a learned Doctor, able to instruct Esculapius himself, for he never obliged Mankind yet with a *Panacœa*, an universal Pill or Powder that could cure all Diseases, which now every Post can direct you to, though it proves only the Hangman's Remedy for all Diseases by Death. *Pudet hæc opprobria dici;* for shame, my dear Countrymen, reassume your Reasons, and expose not your Bodies and Purses to the handling of such illiterate Fellows, who never had the Education of a Grammar-School, much less of an University.

Nor be ye so irrational as to imagine anything extraordinary (unless it be Ignorance) in a Pair of outlandish Whiskers, tho' he's so impudent to tell you he has been Physician to 3 Emperours and 9 Kings when in his own Country he durst not give Physick to a Cobbler.

Nor be gulled with another sort of Impostor, who allures you to him with CURE WITHOUT MONEY, but when he once has got you into his Clutches, he handles you as unmercifully as he does unskilfully.

Nor be ye imposed on by the Pretence of any *Herculean* Medicine, that shall with four Doses at 5s. a Dose, cure the most inveterate Complaint, and Distempers not to be eradicated (in the Opinion of the most learned in all Ages) with less than a Renovation of all the Humours in the whole Body.

These and the like Abuses (too numerous here to be mentioned) have induced me to continue this public Way of Information, that you may be honestly dealt with, and perfectly cured, repairing to him, who with God's Blessing on his Studies and 20 Years successful Practice in this City of London hath attained to the easiest and speediest way of curing.

MARSHALL'S
PREPARED CUBEBS,
A Sure Remedy for CATARRH, COLD in the HEAD, ASTHMA, all DISEASES of the THROAT, Hay-Fever, Foul Breath, &c.
DEPOT,
JAMES B. HORNER,
59 Maiden Lane, N.Y., U.S.A.
Sample box by mail, postage prepaid, on receipt of 25 cents. Sold by Druggists.

American 1880

This curious and suspicious testimonial ran in the "Daily Post" of July 14, 1736.

THESE are to certify, that I Richard Sandford, Waterman, dwelling in Horsely-down-street, near the Dipping Pond, have a Son, who for a considerable Time was troubled with a *Pain in his Stomach, a Sleepiness and Giddiness*, whereupon I calling to Mind that some Years since my Wife's Mother, betwixt 60 and 70 years of Age, *afflicted with a Palsy or Hemeplegia, or loss of the Use of one Side of her Body, had been cured by*

Mr. JOHN MOORE, *Apothecary,*

At the Pestle and Mortar in Laurence-Pountney's Lane, the first Great Gates on the Left-Hand from Cannon-street,

I applied to him for Relief of my Son, who after having taken a few of his Worm-Powders, they brought from him a WORM (or INSECT) like a Hog-Louse, with Legs and hairy, or a Kind of Down all over it, and very probably more, but he going to a common Vault they were lost; upon which he is amended as to his former Illnesses, and I desire this may be printed for the Good of others.

Witness RICHARD SANDFORD.

Oct. 6, 1735.

N.B. The said JOHN MOORE's Worm Medicines and Green-Sickness Powder, are sold at Mrs. Reader's at the Nine Sugar-Loaves, a Chandler's Shop in Hungerford-Market, sealed with his Coat of Arms, being a Cross, with the Words, *John Moore's Worm-Powders*, &c., inscribed round it: And if any are Sold at any place, except at his own House, without that Seal and Inscription, they are Counterfeits.

He sells Byfield's Sal Volatile Oliosum, at 6d. per Ounce.

To be had at the said J. Moore's,

COLUMBARIUM; or, The Pigeon-House: Being an Introduction to a Natural History of Tame Pigeons, giving an Account of the several Species known in England, with the Method of breeding them, their Distempers and Cures.

The two chief Advantages, which a real Acquaintance with Nature brings to our Minds, are first, by instructing our Understandings and gratifying our Curiosities; and next by exciting and cherishing our Devotion. Boyle's Experimental Philosophy, p. 3.

SMOKE MARSHALL'S
PREPARED CUBEB CIGARETTES,
For Catarrh, Cold in the Head, Asthma, Hay Fever, Throat Diseases, &c.

Sold by all Druggists; or send 25 cents for sample box by mail, to

JAMES B. HORNER, 59 Maiden Lane, New York, U. S. A.

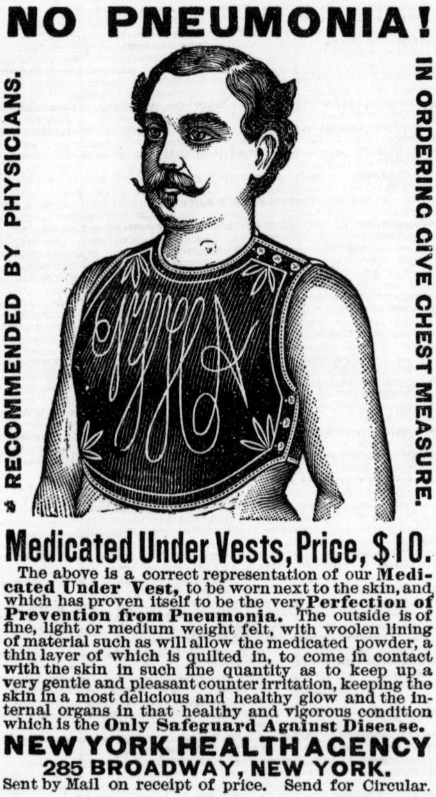

American 1800.

In England in the 1770's Mr. Van Butchell used advertising techniques that caused him to stand above the level of ordinary charlatans of this period. When his wife died, he had her embalmed, and put on display for his patients to see. He made her very useful as a means of publicity, as illustrated by this notice which ran in the "St. James's Chronicle" October, 1776.

> VAN BUTCHELL (not willing to be unpleasantly circumstanced, and wishing to convince some good Minds they have been misinformed) acquaints the Curious no Stranger can see his embalmed Wife, unless (by a Friend or personally) introduced to himself, any Day between Nine and One, Sundays excepted.

One of the most original and creative quacks, Van Butchell didn't miss a trick that would bring him publicity. He painted the following sign across the entire front of his own house and half way across the one next door.

BY
HIS MAJESTY'S
Thus, said sneaking Jack, I'll be first ; if I get my Money, ROYAL speaking like himself, I don't care who suffers.
LETTERS PATENT,
MARTIN
VAN BUTCHELL'S
NEW INVENTED
With caustic care—and old Phim.
SPRING BANDS
AND FASTENINGS
Sometimes in six days, and always in ten—the Fistula in Ano.
FOR
THE APPAREL
AND FURNITURE
July 6.
OF
Licensed to deal in Perfumery, i. e.
HUMAN BEINGS
Hydrophobia cured in thirty days.
AND
BRUTE CREATURES.

One of the biggest advertisers of his time, Van Butchell placed ads in every available paper. The following specimens are taken from various newspapers at various times.

Fistulæ—Patients—Fee—is—according—to ability ! let those—who have much give—without grudging !—(heavy guineas—down : I don't like paper ;—unless—from the Bank of good Old England)—Plain folk—do comply—very readily : so shall—the gaudy :—or keep their complaints ! Many—are in want of food ;—and raiment, for large families. Such—will be made whole—just so speedily as the most wealthy ; that's " one right of man," and he shall have it ; while God grants me health !—(Philosophers—say—Mankind—are equal :—and pure religion—kindly—promotes—good.)

Tender—hearted—Man—User of the Knife,—Would'st thou cut thy Wife? (—Unless two * were by?—Fearing she might die?—) Is—not —Blood—the Life? If the Empress of Russia—the Emperor of Germany—the King of Prussia—an Immaculate,—or the Pope of Rome —were sorely smitten—with bad Fistulæ and tormenting Piles—visited Martin to be made quite whole:—*Without Confinement—Fomentation—Risk—Infection—Poultice—Caustic—or Cutting:* — *bringing* two per Cent. of Five Years Profit.—☞ Less *is* not *his* fee. Nor would he suffer a third person to be in the room. Not wanting help,—he won't be hinder'd; by half-willed spies; slavish informers: nor sad alarmists. All his patients live: and—Jehovah—praise.

To the Editor—of a Morning Paper—*Ego—Secundus.*—Of God every man—hath his proper gift: glory be to him—that of mine is healing: —(Not miraculous,—nor by Satan's aid:)—being vigilant—while gay lads gamed at the Tennis Court—I found it in schools anatomical—Fistulæ and Piles—best my genius fit—Very broad is art—narrow human wit: tho' man was complete (—As he ought to be with an hairy chin.)—Lovely women hate fops effeminate.—Time approaches when among certain men—in another age—beards—will—be—the—rage!

To many I refer—for my character: each will have the grace—to write out his case; soon as he is well—an history tell: for the public good;—so save human blood: as—all—true—folk—shou'd. Sharkish people may—keep themselves away—*Those that use men ill—I never can heal; being forbidden—to cast pearls to pigs; lest—they—turn—and —tear. Wisdom makes dainty: patients come to me, with heavy guineas —between ten and one: but—I—go—to—none.*

Mender of mankind; in a manly way.

This ad for snuff, which was supposed to cure lunacy, ran in the "General Advertiser" on June 21, 1749.

GENTLEMEN,

ONCE more I desire you to remember, I have published my *Imperial Snuff*, for all Disorders in the Head; and I think I might have gone further, and said, for all Disorders of Body and Mind. It hath set a great many to rights that was never expected, but there is but few, or none, that careth to have it published they were a little out of their Senses, although it be really an Ailment that none can help; but there is present Relief, if not a Cure; but I hope both, as by God's Assistance it hath been performed already on many. And I think it my Duty to let the World know it, that they may not bear so many miserable Ailments that is capable of curing. I hear it is reported abroad I am dead, and that the World is imposed on; but, thank God, I am alive and put my Dependance on him, that he will give me leave to do some more Service before I go hence. But suppose I was dead, my Snuff is alive, and I hope it will live after I am dead, as it is capable of keeping the World in sprightly Life and Health, which must be allowed to be the greatest Blessing in the World. But what is Riches without that? And what would some have given for some of these Reliefs before it was advertised. But you are all heartily welcome at this Price of Six-pence, at present, but I should be glad of more from the Rich. I do assure you it is sold at this Price in regard to the Poor only.

I am yours, etc.

SAMUEL MAJOR.

In Swedland Court, against the end of Half-Moon-Alley, Bishopsgate Street.

From the American publication "Harpers Weekly" in the 1880's.

OZONE is nature's disinfectant, and no disease can exist in a malignant form where it is in the atmosphere. It renders sewer gases harmless. In Diphtheria and Scarlatina its effects are wonderful. In Intermittent, Marsh, or Malarial fevers it is of inestimable value, and Fever and Ague cannot exist where there is Ozone. It removes the offensiveness of the sick chamber, filling it with fresh and pleasant odors.

We supply Ozone Generators in two sizes; prices, $3 50 and $5 00. Orders by post promptly attended to. Send for pamphlet. **HEKTOGRAPH CO.,**
22 and 24 Church St., New York.

This handbill was distributed in England in 1734.

WHEREAS it has been of late the Endeavour of several Members of the Physicians College, to reform the Abuses of the Apothecaries, as well in the Prizes as in the Composition of their Medicines, This is to give Notice for the public Good, that a superfine Sort of *Jesuits Bark* ready powder'd and paper'd into Doses, with or without Directions for the Use of it, is to be had at Dr. Charles Goodal's at the Coach and Horses, in Physician's Colledge in Warwick Lane, at 4s. per Ounce, or for a Quantity together at £3 per Pound; for the Reasonableness of which Prizes, (considering the Loss and Trouble in powdering) we appeal to all the Druggists and Apothecaries themselves in Town, and particularly to Mr. Thair, Druggist in Newgate Street, to whom we paid full 9s. per Pound for a considerable Quantity for the Use of our self and our friends.

And for the Excellency and Efficacy of this particular Bark enquire of Dr. Morton in Grey Friars.

I am to be spoken with at Prayers at S. Sepulchre's every Day, *but the Lord's Day, at Seven in the Morning, and at Home from Eight in the Morning till Ten at Night.*

The Poor may have Advice (*that is,* Nothing) *for* Nothing.

From American publications of the 1870's and 80's.

THE CONSTANT ELECTRIC CURRENT,

FROM OUR ELECTRIC GENERATOR,

CURES Headache, Neuralgia, Rheumatism, Pains in the Back, Loins, Limbs, and Kidneys, Extreme Weariness, Nervousness, Incipient Consumption, Piles, Malarial Aches and Pains, Indigestion, Sleeplessness, Debility, Exhaustion, Liver Complaint, and all other *diseases requiring the peculiar stimulation afforded by a constant electric current.* This gentle stimulation of the affected part induces nutrition in that region, and gives nature the aid required to set all of the repairing agencies actively at work.

This powerful yet simple and compact generator develops a continuous, mild electric current, capable of passing entirely through the human body, affecting every organ, nerve, and tissue, producing marked curative effects.

The current, although so subtile and permeating, is not perceptible to the senses, yet it will operate a galvanometer through a resistance of 5,000 ohms, equal to a telegraph line over 300 miles long.

This truly scientific instrument is indorsed by physicians and electricians, and *will cure when all other things fail.*

The Constant Current Electric Generator

with full instructions for use, is sent by mail, on receipt of the price, $3.00, or by express, C. O. D., with collection charges added, with the privilege of examination. *We guarantee safe delivery of the Generator by mail.*

All remittances should be by Postal Money Order, Draft, or Registered Letter.

ONE-HALF SIZE.

PRICE $3.

Fine hard rubber case. Nickel plated binding posts and electrodes. Thoroughly well made and complete. It never gets out of order. ☞ *No acids, no liquids, no trouble.*

CONSTANT CURRENT CURE CO.,

(Incorporated under the laws of the State of New York.) **207 Main St., Buffalo, N. Y.**

From American newspapers of the 1880's.

In a December, 1771, issue of the "Gazetteer," we find this ad placed by Mr. Patence, a benefactor to humanity.

MR Patence, Dentist and Dancing Master, No. 8, Bolt Court, Fleet Street, whose Ingenuity in making artificial Teeth, and fixing them without the least Pain, can be attested by several of the Nobility, and hopes to be honoured by the rest of the Great—may depend his Study shall be devoted to the good of every Individual. His whole Sets, with a Fine enamel on, is a Proof of his excelling all Operators. He charges ten Guineas for a whole, five for an upper or under Set, and half-a-Guinea for a single Tooth.—His Rose Powder for preserving the Teeth, is worthy to grace and perfume the chamber of a Prince.—His Medicines for preventing all Infections and sore Throats have been experienced by several.—As for dancing, he leaves that to the multitude of Ladies and Gentlemen whom he has taught, and desires to be rewarded no more than his Merit deserves, nor no less. Public School nights, Monday, Wednesday, and Friday Evenings; Tuesday Evenings set apart for Cotillons only.—*N.B.* His Rose Dentrifice may be had at Mr Nesbit's Toy Shop Bishopsgate Street, and at his House, at 2s. 6d. the box.

Four years later Mr. Patence published this ad in the "Morning Post." Evidently he was not satisfied with being a dentist and dancing-master, for here we find he has assumed the title of "surgeon by birth."

To the *Nobility*, *Gentry*, and Others.

PATENCE, Surgeon by Birth, and Dentist, having had ten Years Practice, performs every Operation on the Teeth, Gums, &c., with superior Skill, and whose Cures are not excelled or even equalled by any Dentist whatever. And as a Confirmation of the same, please to observe the following :—

October 5. A Gentleman who had lost all his Teeth, his Gums ulcerated and scorbutic, in five Days made a perfect Cure, fixed him in a whole set of natural Teeth, without Springs or any Fastening.

October 16. A Lady whose Jaw was fractured by a Barber, her Teeth loose, her Gums ulcerated, attended with a running Matter, and an inflammation in her Cheeks, with a callous Swelling, cured without poulticing or cutting.

October 20. A Lady that had lost all her upper Teeth by using Powders and Tinctures that are advertised to cure Everything, her Mouth ulcerated, and her Breath nauseous, is now delicately Clean, and replaced the Teeth with those that never change their Colour.

Sunday, October 29. Perfectly relieved a Person that had lost both Palate and Speech ; when he drank or eat it came out at his Nostrils, and had been in that state three Years ; he had applied to Surgeons and several Hospitals, who deemed him incurable, and told him, one and all, he could have no Relief ; he now speaks articulate, eats and drinks with Pleasure, which if any one should doubt, he can refer them to the Man. These, with upwards of three thousand Operations and Cures, have been accomplished by your humble Servant, M. PATENCE.

At No. 403, in the Strand, near *Southampton Street*, London. Where the Teeth, though ever so foul, are made delicately white in six Minutes, and Medicines given for their preservation, for half a Guinea, any hour after ten in the Morning. Advice gratis, and profound Secrecy if required.

☞ Envy may snarl, but superior Abilities assists the Afflicted.

With so many rivals, it is interesting to note the exactness and extra details of the address supplied by most quacks.

IN the Strand, over against the Maypole, on the left Hand coming from Temple-Bar, at the Sign of the Golden Cross, between a Sword Cuttlers and a Milliner's Shop, the Sign of the Sugar Loaf and Barber's Pole, within four Doors of the Mitre Tavern : Where you may see a large Red coloured Lanthorn, with Eleven Candles in it ; and a white Sign written upon with red Letters DUTCH DOCTOR, Licensed by his most Excellent Majesty : and a long Entry with a Hatch and a Knocker on it. Where you may come in privately, and speak with him, and need not be ashamed, he having not any in his House but himself and his Family.

In the mid 1800's a long advertisement telling of the incomparable virtues of Riga Balsam ran in several American newspapers. After all sorts of marvelous claims and statements the ad ends with this postscript.

> N.B. The trial of the Riga Balsam is this : Take a hew or a ram, drive a nail through its skull, brains and tongue, then pour some of it into the wound, it will directly stop the blood and cure the wound in eight or nine minutes, and the creature will eat as before.
>
> A stoop costs two dollars, and it is sold in smaller portions ; at the sale every person gets a direction which describes its surprising virtues and how it is to be used. The glasses, jars and bottles, are sealed up with this seal (A. K. Balsam) to prevent counterfeits.
>
> *Ecclesiasticus*, chap. xxxiii. ver. 4. The Lord hath created medicines out of the earth, and he that is wise will not abhor them.

A close parallel to this product was introduced a century earlier in Holland. The "Dutch Mercurius" of January 1772 carries this story.

"On December the 30th, 1771, Mr. Tunnestrik experimented in the presence of the Prince Stadholder and sundry professors, by driving an iron spike into a horse's head, and afterwards pulling it out with a pair of pincers. Hereupon he poured certain oils by him invented into the wound, by means of which the horse within six minutes was whole again, and not even a scar remained to be seen."

From the American publication "Harper's Weekly" in the 1880's.

QUASSIA, OR BITTER TONIC CUP.

One of the greatest medical benefactors of the day for Sick Headache, Loss of Appetite, Dyspepsia, Fever and Ague, Remittent, Intermittent, and Malarious Fevers, Colic, Sour Stomach, Heartburn, Biliousness, Kidney Complaint, &c. Are made of wood and carried easily in the pocket. They are an invaluable medicine to travellers and people not living near to a doctor. By mail, 25 cents each.

1881 Catalogue, No. 16, Fishing Tackle, 250 Illustrations, by mail, 5 cents.

1881 No. 17 General Catalogue, over 400 Illustrations, by mail, 5 cents.

PECK & SNYDER, 124 Nassau St., N.Y.

From American publications of 1880.

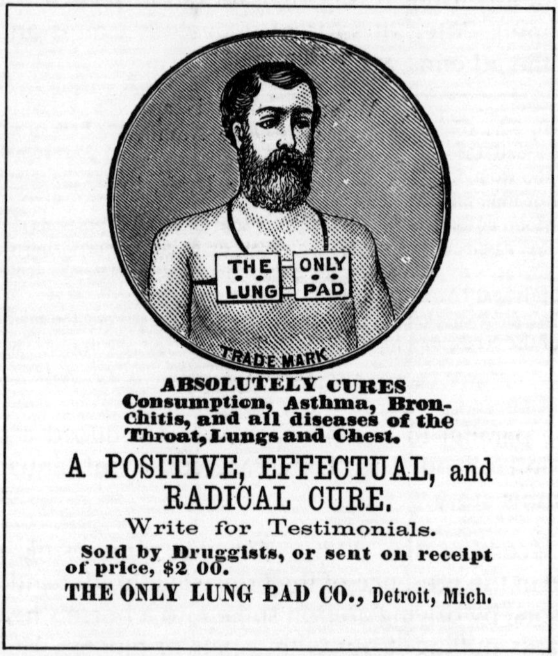

In the mid 1880's a man named Saffold advertised his cure-alls with handbills. The following are two of the many he distributed.

Dear Friends, let your Disease be what God will,
Pray to Him for a Cure, try Saffold's Skill ;
Who may be such a healing Instrument,
As will cure you to your own Heart's Content.
His Medicines are cheap and truly good.
Being full as safe as your daily Food—
Saffold he can do what may be done, by
Either Physick or true Astrology.
His best Pills, rare Elixir and Powder,
Do each Day praise him louder and louder.
Dear Countrymen, I pray be you so wise
When Men backbite him, believe not their Lies,
But go, see him, and believe your own Eyes.
Then he will say you are honest and kind.
Try before you judge and speak as you find.

He knows some who are Knaves in Grain,
And have more Gall and Spleen than Brain,
Will ill reward his Skill and Pain.

He hath practised Astrology above 15 Years, and hath License to practise Physick, and he thanks God for it, hath great Experience and wonderful Success in both those Arts, giving to doubtful People and by God's Blessing, cureth the Sick of any Age or Sex or Distemper though given over by Others, and never so bad (if curable); therefore let none despair of a Cure, but try him.

Yet some conceited Fools will ask how he came to be able to do such great Cures, and to foretell such strange Things, and to know how to make such rare and powerful Medicines, as his best *Pills*, *Elixir* and *Diet Drinks* are, and wherefore he doth publish the same in Print? But he will answer such dark Animals thus:

It hath so pleased God, the King of Heaven,
Being He to him hath Knowledge given,
And in him there can be no greater Sin,
Than to hide his Talent in a Napkin.
His Candle is Light and he will not under
A Bushel put it, let the World wonder:
Though he be traduced by such like Tools,
As have Knaves' Hearts, Lackbrains are Fools.

☞ **I request a favourable Construction upon this Publick way of Practice (And** *as I am a Graduate Physician) should wholly omit to appear in Print, as well in this Disease as I have at all Times in all other Diseases, only in Opposition to the Ignorant, that pretend to Cure, and to prevent the ruine of them that suffer and I see daily throw themselves upon ignorant and outlandish Pretenders and others, to the Patient's utter ruine of Body and Purse.* AND *upon this Consideration alone, I was persuaded rather to adventure the censure of* some, than conceal that which may be of great use to many.

American, 1800's.

MR. MURRAY, of the *Golden Rule*, writes: "I was troubled last winter with an obstinate catarrh, which invaded my throat and lungs, and caused a most trying cough. I have used your Oxy-Hydrogenated Air with *perfect success*, every trace of cough and catarrh having been removed by your truly wonderful treatment.

From the Boston Journal.

Dr. Judge is widely and favorably known as a physician of high reputation. His remedies are highly recommended. Send for pamphlet. Patients at a distance treated by giving description of case.

DR. JUDGE & CO., 79 Beach Street, Boston, Mass.

The Celestial Bed Empire

In the year 1775 in London, a young doctor named Graham began his practice and started to build one of the most extraordinary empires of all time.

Dr. Graham received his medical degree at the University of Athens. He practiced for some time at Pontefract. Then he came to America and traveled as a philanthropic physician. He supposedly administered relief to diseases that had baffled all ordinary physicians. Here he picked up a good deal of experience which he put to the test on his return to England.

Upon returning home, he made an excursion through the country, and according to his own account, was successful in curing many individuals whose cases had been considered desperate. Graham was a well dressed, handsome man with a great fluency of speech, and this helped attract many to him.

In 1775, Graham settled in London and opened a house in Pall Mall across from the King's Palace. Here he specialized in disorders of the ear and eye and advertised to that effect in the daily papers. Although these early ads were mild by comparison to his later productions, they still had an undeniable hint of quackery about them. One of them appeared on February 9, 1776, after stating "that from motives of delicacy the Doctor makes it an invariable rule never on any account to mention the cure, however extraordinary, of any person, poor or rich." He then gives the following particulars of his practice:

> Dr Graham began to practise in London, Feb. 1, 1775, and the following is the general state of his Practice in disorders of the Eye and Ear: from that time to November 1, being a period of nine Months, cures or relieved 281; refused as incurable on their first Application, 317; after a short Trial (by desire) found incurable 47; dismissed for Neglect, etc. 57; country, foreign, and other Patients, events unknown, 381.

The doctor's next step was based on his desire for "the propagation of a much more strong, beautiful, active, healthy, wise and virtuous race of human beings, than the present puny, insignificant, foolish, peevish, vicious and nonsensical race of Christians, who quarrel, fight, bite, devour and cut one another's throats about they know not what." In May, 1779, he opened what was called "The Temple of Health" in the Adelphi. The following is one of the original ads which ran in the "Morning Herald":

TEMPLE OF HEALTH, Adelphi.

To their Excellencies the Foreign Ambassadors, to the Nobility, Gentry, and to Persons of Learning and of Taste.

By Particular Desire, the Exhibitions at the TEMPLE of HEALTH will be continued as usual every TUESDAY, THURSDAY, and SATURDAY Evenings, till the TEMPLE of HYMEN be opened, which will be announced in the Public Papers.

THE CELESTIAL BRILLIANCY of the Mediço-Electrical Apparatus in all the apartments of the Temple, will be exhibited

By Dr. GRAHAM himself

Who will have the honour of explaining the true Nature and Effects of Electricity, Air, Music, and Magnetism when applied to the Human Body.

In the Introductory Oration, the whole Art of enjoying Health and vigour of Body and of Mind, and of preserving and exalting personal beauty and loveliness; or in other words of living with Health, Honour, and Happiness, in this world for at least an hundred years, is pointed out and warmly inculcated. Previous to the display of the Electrical Fire, the Doctor will delicately touch upon the CELESTIAL BEDS which are soon to be opened in the Temple of Hymen, in Pall Mall, for the propagation of Beings, rational and far stronger and more beautiful in mental as well as in bodily Endowments, than the present puny, feeble and nonsensical race of Christians — probationary immortals, which crawl and fret, and cut one anothers throat for nothing at all, on most parts of this terraqueous globe.

This Apparatus which visibly displays, as it were, the various facilities of the material Soul of universal and eternal Nature, is acknowledged by all who have seen it, to be by far the largest, most useful and most magnificent that now is or that ever was in the world. Admittance 5s.

But in order that Persons of every Rank may have a View of this most magnificent Apparatus, the Temple of Health may be viewed every Day this Week, from two o'Clock in the Afternoon till eight at Night. Admittance 1s.

N.B.—A Pamphlet is now published, (by permission) with the particulars of several hundred Cures in confirmed Diseases, lately performed at the Temple of Health, with the Names and Residence of the Patients, at their own particular Desire, to be had of the Porter at the Temple, price only 3d.

As a further attraction to his temple, Graham hired a beautiful young woman and elevated her from the simple capacity of nursemaid to "Vestina, the Rosy Goddess of Health." She presided over the evening lectures, and, according to the ads, assisted "at the display of the Celestial Meteors, and of that sacred Vital Fire over which she watches, and whose application in the cure of diseases, she daily has the honour of directing."

In another of his advertisements, Graham offers to explain "the whole art of enjoying health and vigour of body and mind, and of preserving and exalting personal beauty and loveliness; or, in other words, of living with health, honour, and happiness in this world, for at least a hundred years." One of the means for ensuring this end, according to the doctor, was the constant use of mud baths. In this case the doctor practiced what he preached, for he was often observed immersed in mud up to his chin, accompanied by Vestina. When in the mud baths, she had her hair elaborately dressed in the fashions of the day with flowers, feathers, and ropes of pearls. Graham would wear an equally elaborate wig.

In the spring of 1781 Graham opened the "Temple of Hymen and Celestial Bed" in Pall Mall. The front was ornamented with an enormous gilt sun, a statue of Hygieia, and other attractive emblems. Inside there were suites of rooms with beautiful walls and mirrors in an attempt to convey the effect of an enchanted palace. Paintings, sculpture, vocal and instrumental music, and all the powers of electricity and magnetism were used to further add to the atmosphere.

As a further attraction he hired two men of extraordinary stature, two sons of Anak, whom he dressed in showy clothes and enormous cocked hats. Their job was to distribute handbills from house to house throughout the town. The handbills were typical of the doctor's bombastic style. Here is one of them:

Temple of Health and of Hymen. Pall Mall.

THE LECTURE at the above place having been received by very numerous, polite and brilliant audiences of Ladies and Gentlemen with unbounded applause, it will be repeated This and every Evening this Week; and precisely at 8 o'clock the Gentleman Usher of the Rosy Rod, assisted by the High Priestess, will conduct the rosy, the gigantic, the stupendous Goddess of Health to the Celestial Throne.

The blooming PRIESTESS of the TEMPLE will endeavour to entertain Ladies and Gentlemen of candour and good nature, by reading a Lecture on the simplest and most efficacious means of preserving health, beauty, and personal loveliness, and serene mental brilliancy, even to the extremest old age.

VESTINA, the GIGANTIC! on the Celestial Throne, as the Goddess of Health, will exhibit in her own person, a proof of the all-blessing effects of virtue, temperance, regularity, simplicity, and moderation; and in these luxurious, artificial, and effeminate times, to recommend those great virtues.

The Temple (which exhibits more riches, more elegance, and more brilliancy than any royal Palace in the world) will as usual be sweetly illuminated with wax, in the highest, most dazzling, and most celestial magnificence from 7 till 10 o'clock, This evening and every Evening this week, and the Lecture will begin precisely at eight. Both before and after the Lecture, one of Vestina's Fairy Train will warble forth sweet celestial sounds.—*Admittance only* ONE SHILLING.

The magnificent Electrical Apparatus, and the supremely brilliant and *unique* decorations of this magical Edifice—of this enchanting Elysian Palace! where wit and mirth, love and beauty—all that can delight the soul, and all that can ravish the senses, will hold their court, This and every Evening this week, in chaste and joyous assemblage.

*** Ladies of rank and character are assured, that nothing will be said or seen, which can give even the smallest offence to the chastest and most delicate female eye or ear, and that every thing will be conducted with the most perfect decency and decorum.—Ladies are requested to come early, in order that they may be agreeably accommodated with seats.

*** A very few copies still remaining of Dr. Graham's Private Advisers (*sealed up, price One Guinea*) to those Ladies and Gentlemen who wish to have children, or to become snowy pillars of Health and Beauty, studded as it were with roses, and streaked with celestial blue, may now be had at only Half a Guinea; his other curious and eccentric works, containing full descriptions of his Travels, Discoveries, Improvements, Principles, Cures, Electrical Apparatus, etc.—formerly 3s. 6d., now only 1s. 9d., and VESTINA, the rosy Goddess's warm Lecture, price 2s. 6d.

The most important feature of the doctor's establishment was the Celestial Bed. This wonder-working piece of furniture was made by a tinman named Denton (who was later convicted of counterfeiting). The bed was said to cost 12,000 pounds, and was beautifully carved and gilded. It was covered with the finest silks, supported by twenty-eight glass pillars and surmounted by a richly carved and gilded canopy, from which crimson silk curtains with fringe and tassels were suspended. Graham contended that married couples without children would have heirs by sleeping in this bed. The charge was one hundred pounds per night, and he had numerous wealthy customers.

> **TEMPLE OF HEALTH AND HYMEN,**
> **PALL MALL,**
> *Near the King's Palace.*
>
> IF there be one human Being, rich or poor, Male or Female, or of the doubtful Gender, in or near this great Metropolis of the World, who has not had the good Fortune and the Happiness of hearing the celebrated Lecture, and of seeing the grand celestial Bed, the magnificent electrical Apparatus, and the supremely brilliant and unique Decorations of this magical Edifice, of this enchanting Elysian Palace! —where Wit and Mirth, Love and Beauty—all that can delight the Soul and all that can ravish the Senses—will hold their Court, this, and every Evening this week, in chaste and joyous Assemblage—let them now come forth, or for ever afterwards let them blame themselves and bewail their irremediable Misfortune.

About the bed Graham had this to say, "Nothing is more surprising than the truly divine energy of this celestial and electric fire, which fills every part of the bed, as well as the magnetic fluid, both of them calculated to give the necessary degree of strength and exertion to the nerves. Besides the melodious tones of the harmonica, the soft sounds of a flute, the charms of an agreeable voice, and the harmonious notes of the organ, being all joined, how can the power and virtue of such a happy conjunction fail in raising sentiments of admiration and pleasure in the soul of the philosopher, and even of the physician?"

Graham would also advise married couples to sing. "Music," he said, "softens the mind of a happy couple, makes them all love, all harmony; their bodies, their souls unite, their existence is melted into a single being, which yields itself up with rapture to divine transports, and loses itself in an Elysium of bliss. In this state, this incessantly progressive enjoyment, the happy couple imagine themselves raised above this world, and become inhabitants of a superior region." Thus he continued until coming to the last and principal part of his talks, "When the preliminary regimen which I have just described has been scrupulously observed and followed, and a new vigour has been acquired by drinking of the divine balm, which for the benefit of the human race, I have concocted with my own hand, and which, however, costs only a guinea a bottle, and when all these means have not proved sufficient for arriving at the end proposed, the last must then be absolutely applied to, that most extraordinary expedient which I alone possess, and which cannot fail. This agent is a most marvelous celestial bed, which I call magnetico-electric; it is the first, the only one in the world, or that ever existed. It is placed on the second floor, in a large and elegant hall, on the right hand of my orchestra, and immediately before my charming hermitage. In a neighbouring closet is placed a cylinder by which I communicate the celestial fire to the bed-chamber, that fluid which animates and vivifies all, and those cherishing vapours and Oriental perfumes, which I convey thither by means of tubes of glass. The celestial bed rests on massy and transparent columns; coverings of purple, and curtains of celestial blue surround it, and the bed-clothes are perfumed with the most costly essences of Arabia; it is exactly similar to those that adorn the palaces in Persia, and to that of the favorite sultana in the seraglio of the Grand Turk. This bed is the fruit of the most laborious industry, and of the most indefatigable zeal. I will not mention the sums it has cost me: they are immense. I shall only add that I have omitted none of those precautions which decency and delicacy have a right to exact. Neither I, nor any of my people, are entitled to ask who are the persons that rest in this chamber, which I have denominated the Holy of Holies. This bed is never shown to those who come only to view the accessory parts. This precaution is as proper as it is delicate; for is there a being frigid enough to resist the influence of that pleasure, of those transports which this enchanting place inspires? It furnishes the grossest imagination with the means of refining its enjoyments, of multiplying its pleasures, and of carrying them to their highest degree. But the consequences are cruel; such dangerous refinements on the pleasures of the senses abridge the period of life, and relax the springs both of body and mind. Persons, however, who would penetrate to this throne of pleasure, are intended to signify their desire to me in writing, and having appointed the night, and enclosed a bank-bill for one hundred pounds, I shall furnish them with an admission ticket."

As the temple and bed grew more famous and more visitors came, Graham added to the luxury and magnificence of the palace. But by March 1784 the farce was played out, the Temple of Health was shut, and all the paraphernalia which had cost so much money, including the famous bed itself, were sold at public auction.

Graham's expenses were very heavy, and when his advertisements failed to draw, he fell into poverty, and is said to have died soon afterward in Glasgow.

New Ideas and Inventions

From the English newspaper "Mercurius Politicus", December 1660.

MOST Excellent and Approved *Dentifrices* to scour and cleanse the Teeth, making them white as Ivory, preserves from the Toothach; so that, being constantly used, the parties using it are never troubled with the Toothach; it fastens the Teeth, sweetens the Breath, and preserves the mouth and gums from Cankers and Imposthumes. Made by *Robert Turner*, Gentleman; and the right are onely to be had at *Thomas Rookes*, Stationer, at the Holy Lamb at the East end of St Pauls Church, near the School, in sealed papers, at 12d. the paper.

The Reader is desired to beware of counterfeits.

From American newspapers of 1818.

St. Louis (Missouri Territory) North America.
April 10, A.D. 1818.

TO ALL THE WORLD.—I declare the earth to be hollow, and habitable within; containing a number of concentric spheres, one within the other, and that their poles are open twelve or sixteen degrees. I pledge my life in support of this truth, and am ready to explore the concave, if the world will support and aid me in the undertaking.

JOHN CLEVES SYMMES
of Ohio, late Captain of Infantry.

I ask one hundred brave companions, well equipped, to start for Siberia, in autumn, with reindeer and sledges, on the ice of the frozen sea. I engage we find a warm country and rich land, stocked with thrifty vegetables and animals, if not men, on reaching about sixty-nine miles northward of latitude 82°. We will return in the succeeding spring.—J. C. S.

A London merchant named Edwards brought the first bag of coffee into England. His Greek servant, after tasting the new brew, decided to start his own business and opened the first coffee-house in 1652. The following is a reprint of the original handbill.

THE VERTUE OF THE COFFEE DRINK,

First made and publicly sold in England by

PASQUA ROSEE.

The grain or berry called coffee, groweth upon little trees only in the deserts of Arabia. It is brought from thence and drunk generally throughout all the Grand Seignour's dominions. It is a simple, innocent thing, composed into a drink, by being dried in an oven, and ground to powder, and boiled up with spring water, and about half a pint of it to be drunk fasting an hour before, and not eating an hour after, and to be taken as hot as can possibly be endured; the which will never fetch the skin of the mouth, or raise any blisters by reason of that heat.

The Turk's drink at meals and other times is usually water, and their diet consists much of fruit; the acidities whereof are very much corrected by this drink.

The quality of this drink is cold and dry; and though it be a drier; yet it neither heats nor inflames more than hot posset. It so incloseth the orifice of the stomach, and fortifies the heat within, that it is very good to help digestion; and therefore of great use to be taken about three or four o'clock afternoon, as well as in the morning. It much quickens the spirits, and makes the heart lightsome; it is good against sore eyes, and the better if you hold your head over it and take in the steam that way. It suppresseth fumes exceedingly, and therefore is good against the head-ache, and will very much stop any defluxion of rheums that distil from the head upon the stomach, and so prevent and help consumptions and the cough of the lungs.

It is excellent to prevent and cure the dropsy, gout, and scurvy. It is known by experience to be better than any other drying drink for people in years, or children that have any running humours upon them, as the king's evil, &c. It is a most excellent remedy against the spleen, hypochondriac winds, and the like. It will prevent drowsiness, and make one fit for business, if one have occasion to watch, and therefore you are not to drink of it after supper, unless you intend to be watchful, for it will hinder sleep for three or four hours.

It is observed that in Turkey, where this is generally drunk, that they are not troubled with the stone, gout, dropsy, or scurvy, and that their skins are exceeding clear and white. It is neither laxative nor restringent.

Made and Sold in St Michael's Alley, in Cornhill, by Pasqua Rosee, at the sign of his own head.

From a weekly New York newspaper of the 1880's.

The Health Jolting Chair

COPYRIGHT.

The most important Health Mechanism ever produced

A Practical Household Substitute for the Saddle-Horse.

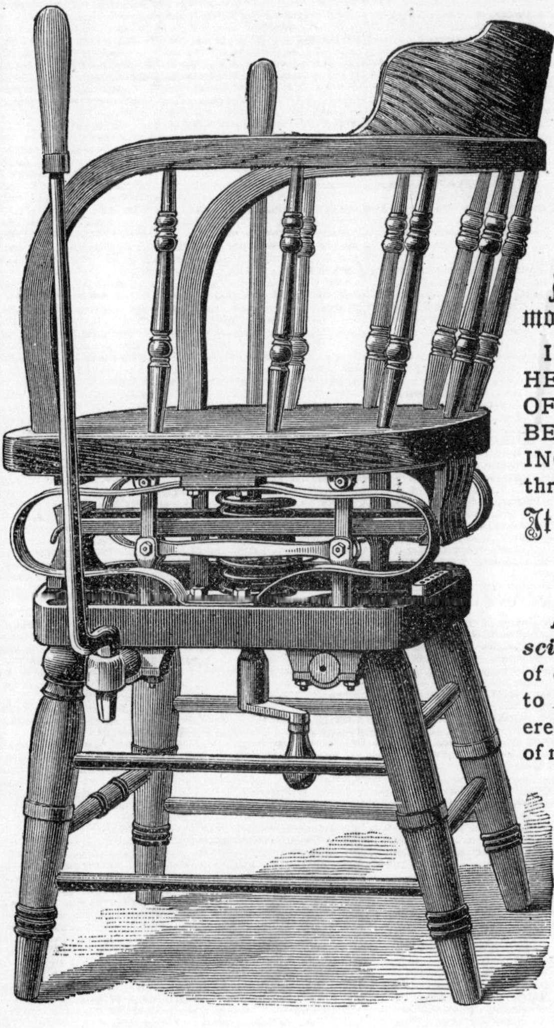

It affords a PERFECT means of giving EFFICIENT exercise to the ESSENTIALLY IMPORTANT NUTRITIVE ORGANS OF THE BODY in the most DIRECT, CONVENIENT, COMFORTABLE, and INEXPENSIVE manner.

Suitable for all ages and for most physical conditions.

INDISPENSABLE TO THE HEALTH AND HAPPINESS OF MILLIONS OF HUMAN BEINGS WHO MAY BE LIVING SEDENTARY LIVES through choice or necessity.

It preserves Health, cures Disease, and prolongs Life.

An ***ingenious, rational, scientific, mechanical*** means of overcoming those impediments to the taking of proper exercise, erected by the artificial methods of modern society.

For certain classes of invalids a veritable Treasure-Trove.

A CONSERVATOR of NERVOUS ENERGY.

No dwelling-house is completely furnished without The Health Jolting Chair.

(CONTINUED ON NEXT PAGE)

USES OF THE

HEALTH JOLTING CHAIR

1st. It strengthens the action of the *heart*, and increases the force of the whole circulation.

2d. It increases the depth and frequency of the *respiratory* movements, promoting oxygenation.

3d. It affords a method of giving local exercise to those great and essentially important internal nutritive organs of the body, the *stomach, intestines, liver, kidneys*, etc. A nutritive stimulant.

4th. It strengthens the muscles of the whole of the trunk and neck; and also especially develops those of the arms, shoulders, and chest, with a minimum strain on the heart and other muscles.

5th. It improves the *general nutrition* of the body in a remarkable manner, and is thus an invaluable PREVENTIVE OF DISEASE. Disease germs do not affect healthy tissues.

6th. It CURES **Constipation, Dyspepsia,** the effects of **Torpid Liver** *and* **Kidneys, Nervous Prostration, Melancholia, Anæmia, General Debility, Loss of Appetite, Sleeplessness, Rheumatism, Gout, Neuralgia,** and many other morbid conditions that may have been the result of a lack of nerve force and circulation of the blood directed to the abdominal and pelvic organs, as well as from deficient heart and respiratory action. A mechanical laxative, diuretic and tonic. It saves time, money, and health. **A household blessing.**

7th. It is a **brain-refresher** for those engaged in literary and other mental work, and is a great remedy for the **tired voice** of voice-users. Unlike most medication, it *creates* VITAL FORCE.

8th. In conjunction with a regulated diet it will cure **Corpulency,** without pedestrial strain.

9th. It is invaluable for rainy-day exercise for children and adults, or for occasions when it is too hot, or too cold, or when out-of-door exercise is otherwise climatically (or socially) undesirable.

WHO SHOULD USE THE HEALTH JOLTING CHAIR.

All Persons *should use it whose sedentary habits have caused or may cause disease.* This includes many millions of the human family, especially females. It will be found of prime interest as affording a practical means of giving *vigorous* exercise to the **Blind**; to those **Crippled** from paralysis or other causes; to the **Aged, Weak, and Convalescents**; to the **Insane**; and to those afflicted with organic Heart and Pulmonary disorders. Its trade mark, VIS PRESERVATRIX, truly a sustaining, preserving power.

It is a **perfect** *mechanism, constructed in the very best manner; is simple, durable, and its action is wonderfully effective.* We will be pleased to send free to any address an interesting pamphlet relating to the subject, entitled, "*Exercise of the Internal Organs of the Body Necessary to Health.*" For sale by furniture and house-furnishing goods dealers: and by the *sole manufacturers*,

THE HEALTH JOLTING CHAIR COMPANY,
150 West 23d Street, New York.

WONDERFUL

LUNG EXPANDER.

More Fun and Satisfaction for 39c. than was ever seen before.

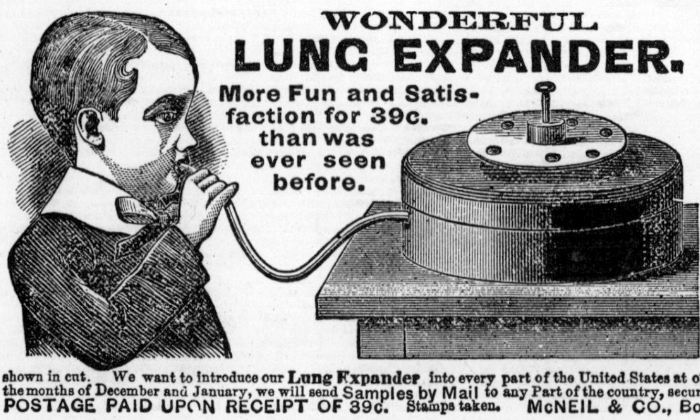

It will **test the capacity of the Lungs.** as accurately as a $50,00 lung testing machine. **NOTHING LIKE IT; EVERYBODY BUYS IT.** More than one half of the human family are troubled, with some kind of **Lung Disease,** a large portion of which is caused by a lack of **Regular and proper exercise of the Lungs.** People soon tire of nauseating medicine but they never tire of healthful exercise mixed with fun and amusement. Our Lung **Expander** stimulates friendly contests among **old and young** alike, and there is a great deal of fun in deciding **who** has the **strongest lungs.** We have made the price so low that every family can afford to have one. The Expander is made of metal, handsomely decorated, and is operated by **blowing through a rubber tube,** as shown in cut. We want to introduce our **Lung Expander** into every part of the United States at once. Special Offer. During the months of December and January, we will send Samples by Mail to any Part of the country, securely packed in a strong box.

POSTAGE PAID UPON RECEIPT OF 39c. Stamps taken. **McNEIL & CO., Box 283, 21 Tyron Row, N.Y.**

One of the first politically inspired products, advertised in the English publication "New Observator" on July 17, 1689.

ORANGE CARDS, representing the late King's reign and expedition of the Prince of Orange; viz. The Earl of Essex Murther, Dr Otes Whipping, Defacing the Monument, My Lord Jeferies in the West hanging of Protestants, Magdalen College, Trial of the Bishops, Castle Maine at Rome, The Popish Midwife, A Jesuit Preaching against our Bible, Consecrated Smock, My Lord Chancellor at the Bed's feet, Birth of the Prince of Wales, The Ordinare Mass-house pulling down and burning by Captain Tom and his Mobile, Mortar pieces in the Tower, The Prince of Orange Landing, The Jesuits Scampering, Father Peter's Transactions, The fight at Reading, The Army going over to the Prince of Orange, Tyrconnel in Ireland, My Lord Chancellor in the Tower. With many other remarkable passages of the Times. To which is added the efigies of our Gracious K. William & Q. Mary, curiously illustrated and engraven in lively figures, done by the performers of the first Popish Plot Cards. Sold by Donnan Newman, the publisher and printer of the New Observator.

The following advertisements ran in American publications of the 1870's and 80's.

The following are the MOST PROMINENT points of SUPERIORITY of

"THE ADAMS & WESTLAKE Wire Gauze Non-Explosive Oil Stove"

OVER ALL OTHERS:

1st.—*Cast-Iron* Base, with *galvanized sheet-iron bottom.*
2d.—Wire-Gauze *inside* the Reservoir, on the same principle as the Sir Humphrey Davy Miners' Lamp (used in this stove only), making it absolutely Non-Explosive.
3d.—*The wick tubes are adjustable,* making it easy to get at the wick, should one be turned below the ratchet.
4th.—Our *Patent "Perforated Box,"* which is much more durable than the ordinary "Perforated Plate." With this Perforated Box more perfect combustion is obtained, the flame is steadied, and not easily affected by draughts of air.
5th.—High chimneys and improved cones, producing a wider and higher flame; hence, more heat.
6th.—The manner of lighting from the front without removing the Drum, having no opening in the Drum to let the cold air rush in and up against the vessels.
7th.—Our Patent Two-Hole Top, by which *several* operations may be performed at one time. The *oven may occupy one side, and baking done, while a large and small vessel occupy the other.*
8th.—The Cornwall Patent Broiler, which is sold with this Stove only.
9th.—Our Flat-Iron Heaters are made to fit Mrs. Potts' Patent Irons.
10th.—A very superior oven. Grates inside may be raised or lowered.
11th.—Superior workmanship and finish.

THE ADAMS & WESTLAKE M'F'G CO., Chicago.

PRINCIPAL AGENCIES:

THE HOME VAPOR BATH AND DISINFECTOR COMPANY,

12 East 23d Street, Madison Square, New York.

The following testimonials to the efficiency of the Home Vapor Bath will sustain what is claimed for it, that it is an important hygienic and sanitary improvement, ever ready to render valuable assistance in case of disease, and a luxurious comfort in one's own home. The apparatus, simple in all its appurtenances and in its operation, is made available to all, as it can easily be attached to any bath-tub in any dwelling provided with the ordinary hot-water kitchen boiler, without in any way interfering with the baths hitherto in use in our homes.

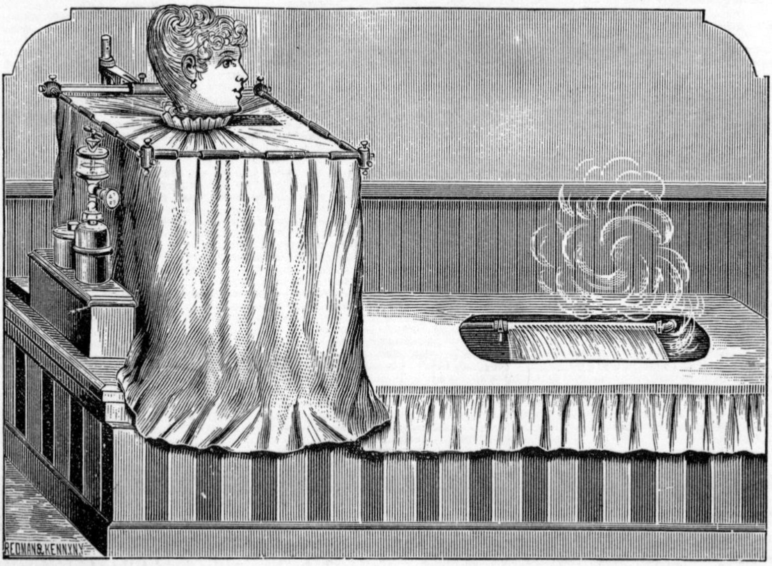

74 West 47th Street,
New York, Nov. 7, 1885.

TO THE HOME VAPOR BATH AND DISINFECTOR CO.:

Gents,—It affords me a great deal of pleasure to express my entire satisfaction with the bath put by you in my residence, 74 West 47th Street. I had been suffering for the past six (6) months from rheumatism, particularly in the knees. After taking three of your vapor baths, I find that I am able to move about freely, and the pains have entirely subsided. I am pleased to be able to write thus, and thanking you for having called my attention to this valuable invention,

I am, gentlemen, yours very truly,

SYLVESTER KNIGHT.

2637 Prairie Avenue,
Chicago, Nov. 16, 1885.

HOME VAPOR BATH CO., 12 EAST 23d STREET, NEW YORK:

Gentlemen,—I have used your apparatus about eight months with entire satisfaction. It has more than met my expectations, and is, I think, a perfect Russian bath. I intended arranging my bath-room as a miniature Turkish and Russian bath establishment, but my attention being called to your apparatus, I was saved that expense, and have, I believe, an arrangement fully as efficacious and satisfactory.

I would not be without it.

Sincerely,

T. R. BURCH.

W. S. BLUNT'S

IMPROVED

UNIVERSAL FORCE PUMPS.

Fig 32

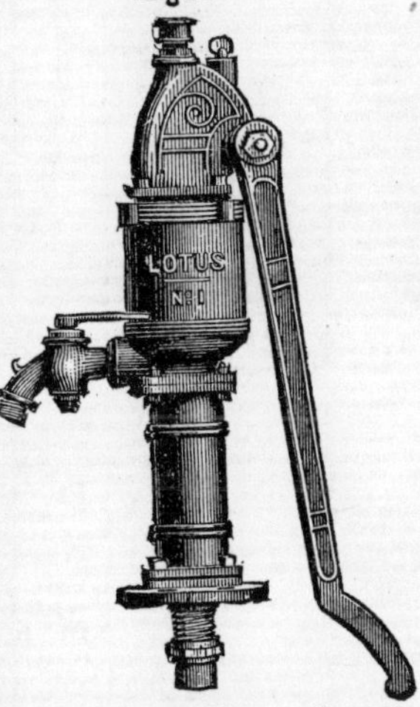

The undersigned begs to offer a new line of the above Pumps, which combine all the improvements that a long experience has suggested. These Pumps have an increased stroke, greater power, superior finish, and beauty of design. They can be placed in any desired position, as the working head rotates. The upper nozzle offers a straight waterway through the Pump, saving much friction when filling a tank. Hose can be used at either nozzle if desired.

A full assortment of these Pumps constantly on hand, for the house and for out-door wells of the greatest depth. For power and reliability, these Pumps cannot be surpassed.

Complete outfits furnished to order, and advice given on all questions relating to water supply. Send for circulars.

94 Beekman St., New York. Eastern Depot: A. M. Morton & Co., Boston, Mass. Depot on Pacific Coast: Dunham, Carrigan & Co., San Francisco, Cal.

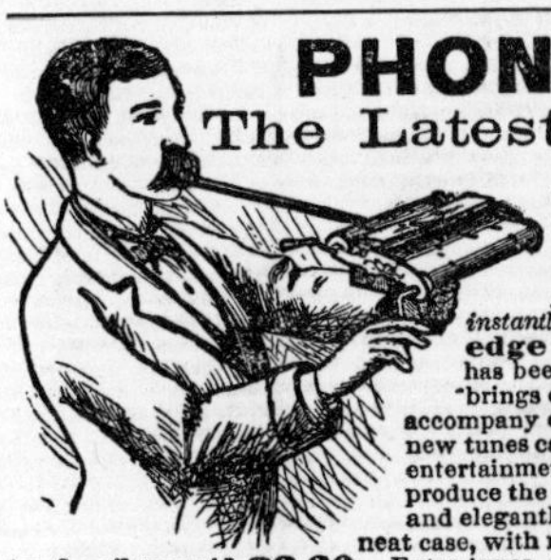

PHONOGRAPHIC CORNET.

The Latest and Greatest Musical Wonder.

The Phonographic Cornet is the latest invention in the musical line. The action of this instrument is almost marvellous. It plays the most complicated airs equal to a first-class Cornet solo. The picture represents the manner of playing: simply turning the little crank on the side produces most exquisite music. The music-producers are genuine first-class Organ Reeds, and the music itself is like that of a first-class Organ played on the high notes, with the flute stops out. *Any tune that ever was written can be instantly played on the Phonographic Cornet,* **without any instruction or knowledge of music whatever** *by the operator.* **A little strip of paper in which the tune has been perforated, is placed in the instrument, and then simply turning the little handle brings out the tune in a clear and extremely melodious manner. Selections of choice music accompany each "cornet." Any child can play this instrument; the music is very pleasing; all the new tunes can be easily obtained, and no musical instrument in the world can provide more genuine entertainment, at home or in company, than the Phonographic Cornet. Anyone can play it, and produce the latest music in a manner that will surprise everyone. The instruments are all strongly and elegantly made of fancy woods, ebonized trimmings, and silvered bolts. They are packed in a neat case, with music strips, directions, &c., &c., and sent by express to any address for $3;** *by registered mail, prepaid,* **$3.30.** Extra tunes, comprising all the latest popular music, are now ready.

Address **THE MASSACHUSETTS ORGAN CO., 43 Washington Street, Boston, Mass.**

SUNK!

STATE OF FLORIDA

"There was nothing wanting to make it a soul-harrowing narrative of a terrible loss of life at sea."—*N. Y. Herald.*

The recent sinking of this immense iron-armored Steamship into the Atlantic affords another distressing proof (the eighth in one month) that *positive safety* does not accompany an ocean voyage even in clear weather and on calm sea. Persons contemplating a European tour, and all other travellers on the water, will do well to send 3c. stamp for manual containing SAFETY PRECAUTION FOR OCEAN travellers. This is no plan for soliciting insurance, but a practical means for the saving of life. Address

JOS. G. KITCHELL, President,
United States L.P. Company. 35 Broadway, New York.

GENTLEMEN'S

BOSTON GARTER.

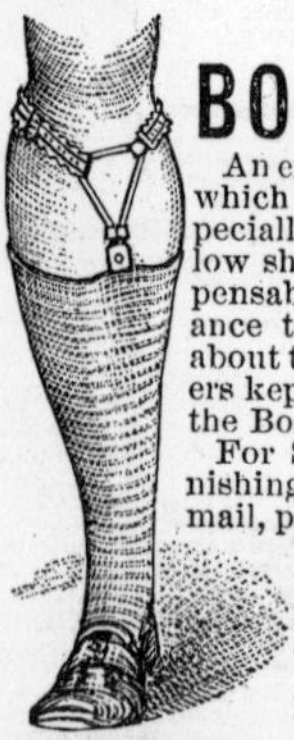

An exceedingly useful invention, without which no gentleman's dress is complete, especially during the summer months, when low shoes are worn, and when it is indispensable to one's comfort and neat appearance to have the stocking fit smoothly about the ankle and the slack of the drawers kept confined at the knees, all of which the Boston Garter accomplishes.

For Sale by all the leading Gents' Furnishing Houses, or Sample will be sent by mail, postage prepaid, on receipt of price.

COTTON, 25c. per pair; SILK, 75c. per pair; SILK (*with pair Sleeve Elastics to match, clasps handsomely nickeled and polished*), $1.25 per set.

Remit by P.O. Order or registered letter. *Mention this paper.* Address

GEORGE FROST & CO., 289 Devonshire St., Boston.

POCKET MOSQUITO BAR

(Holden's Patent).

No discomfort in wearing day or night. No trouble to put on; convenient to carry.

Try one, unless you are mosquito proof. For sale by the trade. Sample sent by mail on receipt of $1.25.

THOS. KANE & CO.,
CHICAGO., ILL.

COLUMBIA TRICYCLES.

Stanch, Reliable, Light, Easy-Running, Finest Materials, Skilful Workmanship, Beautifully Finished, Every Part Interchangeable. So adjustable that the same machine can be ridden by any size of rider. Price, $160. With Columbia Power-Gear, which enables the rider to instantly increase the leverage, and easily ride up steep grades and over rough places, $180.

Send stamp for Illustrated (36 p.) Catalogue.

THE POPE MFG. CO.,
597 Washington St., - - BOSTON, MASS.

THE DESK OF THE AGE.

The Wooton Cabinet Office Secretary.

One hundred and ten compartments all under one lock and key. For full particulars send 3c. stamp.

Wooton Desk Manufacturing Co.,
Indianapolis, Ind., U. S. A.

A Complete Working Telephone.

Cheap enough for a toy, and good enough for practical use. Warranted to work a mile. Samples, with full directions, by express, with 100 feet of wire, for $1 00; or by mail, postpaid, $1 25; extra wire, 25c. per 100 feet.

Address **PECK & SNYDER,**
Dealers in Novelties and Sporting Goods,
P.O. Box 2751. **124 and 126 Nassau St., N. Y.**

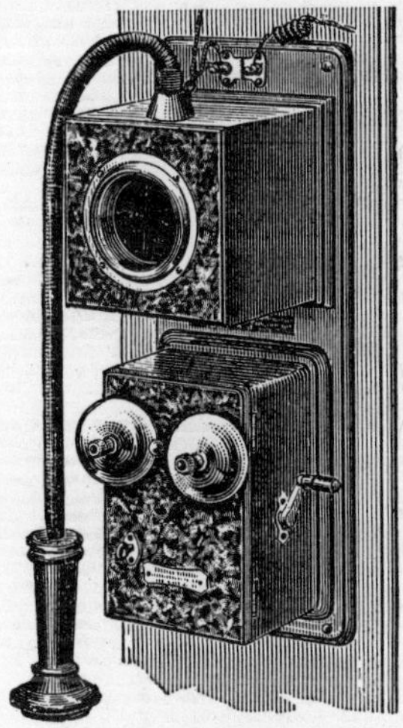

TELEPHONES
For Short Private Lines,
MAGNETO CALL-BELLS, Etc.
Our Instruments unequalled in every particular. Require no Battery. Easily placed in operation. *Send for New Catalogue and Price-List.*
BENNETT TELEPHONE CO.,
Indianapolis, Ind.
Mention this Paper.

HOLCOMB'S NEW AMPLIFYING TELEPHONES
FOR PRIVATE LINES.

The latest and best. Patented April 26th, 1881. These new instruments embody recent and important improvements. They transmit conversation, music, orders, &c., with almost electric speed and surprising fidelity. The only durable and reliable substitute for the Electric Telephones. Work 2 miles. Price $10 per set. Illustrated Circulars Free.

HOLCOMB & CO.,
Mallet Creek, O.

[*Mention this paper.*]

EYESIGHT BY MAIL.

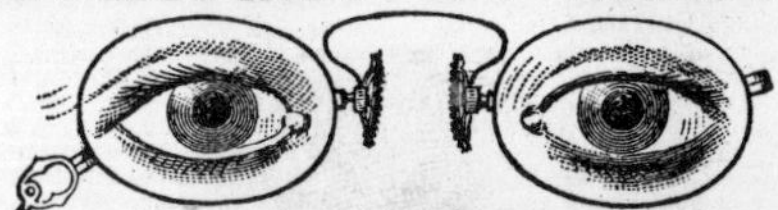

Eyes which do not perform their duty should be assisted by the most carefully made spectacles and eye-glasses, fitted by persons of known and well-tried skill. We send to any address our pamphlet giving a description of every good style of spectacle and eye-glass, and also our book of test types and questions, the answers to which will enable us to fit the glasses with great accuracy. Correspondence regarding the sight will receive careful attention.

JAMES W. QUEEN & CO.,
OPTICIANS,
924 Chestnut Street, Philadelphia.

KING TOILET PACKAGE!

When one sheet is used another presents itself. Most economical and convenient package made. For sale by Druggists and Paper Dealers. Samples sent express paid for $1.00 as follows: New England and Middle States 5 packages with one holder. Other States 4 packages and one holder. Each package guaranteed 800 sheets.

MORGAN ENVELOPE CO.,
Springfield, Mass.

OUR NEW MAGIC LANTERN is a useful and instructive complete instrument, and for Beauty, Accuracy in Operating and Price, cannot be beat. We give Lamp, Chimney, Wick, Reflector, Show Bill, Tickets, 12 Slides with 60 colored li'e like Pictures and Illustrated book of Instruction, packed complete in box for $2.50.

We send our New Catalogue, 228 pages, 2,000 Illustrations of Games, Tricks, Gymnasium Goods, Pase Ball, Tennis, Skates, New Novelties and Holiday Presents, &c., by mail for 15 cents.

PECK & SNYDER, 126–130 NASSAU STREET, N. Y.

45 sold in '88
2,288 sold in '89
6,268 sold in '90
20,049 sold in '91
60,000 will be sold in '92

A Steel Windmill and Steel Tower every 3 minutes.
☞ These figures tell the story of the ever-growing, ever-going, everlasting Steel Aermotor. Where one goes others follow, and we "take the country."

Though sold, we were unable to make all of the 20,049 Aermotors in '91. Orders often waited 8 weeks to be filled, but now we have vastly increased our plant and are prepared promptly to plant our increase in every habitable portion of the globe.

Are you curious to know how the **Aermotor Co.** in the 4th year of its existence, came to make **many times as many windmills as all other makers combined?** How we came to originate the Steel Wheel, the Steel Fixed Tower, the Steel Tilting Tower?

1st. We commenced in a field in which there had been no *improvement for 25 years*, and in which there seemed no talent or ambition, and none has yet been shown except in *feeble* **imitation of our inventions.**

2d Before commencing the manufacture, exhaustive scientific investigation and experiments were made by a skilled mechanical engineer, in which over 5,000 dynamometric tests were made on 61 different forms of wheels, propelled by artificial and therefore uniform wind, which settled definitely many questions relating to the proper speed of wheel, the best form, angle, curvature and amount of sail surface, the resistance of air to rotation, obstructions in the wheel, such as heavy wooden arms, obstructions before the wheel, as in the vaneless mill, and many other more abstruse, though not less important questions. **These investigations proved that the power of the best wind wheels could be doubled, and the AERMOTOR daily demonstrates it has been done.**

3d. To the liberal policy of the Aermotor Co., that guarantees its goods satisfactory or pays freight both ways, and to the enormous output of its factory which enables it to furnish the best article at less than the poorest is sold for. For '92 we furnish the **most perfect bearings** ever put in a windmill, and have made an **exhaustive revision of the Aermotor and Towers.**

If you want a strong, stiff, Steel **Fixed** Tower—or if you want the tower you don't have to climb (the Steel **Tilting** Tower) and the Wheel that runs when all others stand still that costs you less than wood and lasts ten times as long (The Steel Aermotor) or if you want a Geared Aermotor to churn, grind, cut feed, pump water, turn grindstone and saw wood, that does the work of 4 horses at the cost of one ($100), write for copiously illustrated printed matter, showing every conceivable phase of windmill construction and work, to the **AERMOTOR CO.** 12th and Rockwell Sts., Chicago, or 12 Main St., San Francisco.

GALVANIZED It is not enough to make portions of a wheel of galvanized metal. That leaves exposed edges and is not so good as painting. The Steel Aermotor and Steel Tower are now galvanized after being completed, thus **absolutely protected** from rust and decay.

The Aermotor Pneumatic Water Supply System enables you to supply every part of your house with water without an Elevated Tank.

THE PRESIDENT LAWN MOWER.

The most beautiful and perfect Mower ever offered. A complete assortment of **Ten Sizes.** Hand machines, $10 and upward. Handsome New Pony Mower, $55. Horse Mowers, $80 and upward. Acknowledged at home and abroad the Lawn Mower *par excellence. Easily operated*, **noiseless,** and incomparably the most durable. No implement requires so much precision in manufacture as the Lawn Mower: therefore compare the President with all others and **Buy the Best.**

CARR & HOBSON, 47 Cliff St., { *Two Doors from Fulton.*

THE HAMMOND,

The only type-writer awarded a Gold Medal at the New Orleans Exposition.

Constant use does not and cannot disturb its alignment.

The automatic hammer stroke gives absolutely uniform impression. It is unsurpassed in speed, and will write over 600 characters in one minute. Its type wheels, comprising different styles of type, are interchangeable. It manifolds well. Its open carriage ends admit paper of any width. It is light, portable, strong, simple, and durable.

For pamphlet and specimen of writing, address

THE HAMMOND TYPE-WRITER CO.,
143 Centre Street, New York.

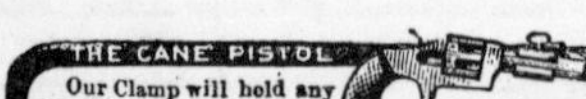

Our Clamp will hold any revolver to a cane. The cane can be held steady, like a gun, to the shoulder. No other fire-arm is so handy or gives such sport as the Cane Pistol.

For hunters, farmers, tourists, young folks, etc. Clamp sent for 50 cts., or 3 for $1. Dealers Supplied. Agents Wanted.
I. KINNEY & CO.,
198 Jefferson Ave., Detroit, Mich.

Full-Sitz, &c. in one. **THE UNIVERSAL BATH.** Vapor & Water, fresh & salt.

PRICE REDUCED. *Many long in use.* Old Baths renewed.
Send for Circulars. **E. J. KNOWLTON, Ann Arbor, Mich.**

$100

PHAETON.

Three Springs; two 3-leaf, 34x1¼ inch back, one 3-leaf, 36x1¼ inch front; *coach axles;* wheels 40x48; wood or patent hubs: 1 inch axle; steel bow tops, with leather roof and side curtains, leather quarters, back stays, and *back curtain;* plain black painting on bodies, fine line stripe on gear; *cloth backs and cushions*, lamps, and Fenders.

These Phaetons are hung low, are very roomy, and are specially adapted to persons requiring comfort and ease in riding. We know of no vehicle built for same price worthy of comparison. Guaranteed to be all as represented. Will be delivered Free on board cars, New York. Terms cash. Reasonable credit given to responsible parties desiring to buy on time. Address

THE EDMISTON & WADDELL COMPANY, Brooklyn E. D., N. Y.

THE BRADLEY TWO-WHEELER

Send for Free Circular "How to purchase direct from the manufacturer." Address

Absolutely free from Horse Motion.

BRADLEY & CO. **SYRACUSE, N. Y.**
22 COLLEGE PLACE, NEW YORK.
32 S. MARKET ST., BOSTON.

Dr. WARNER'S Health Underwear,

MADE OF TWO QUALITIES,
Selected CAMEL'S HAIR and
Pure NATURAL WOOL.

Five Reasons for Wearing the Health Underwear.

1st. Camel's Hair and Wool are twice as warm as the same weight of Cotton or Linen.

2d. They protect the body against excessive heat and against drafts and sudden changes of temperature.

3d. They are an important protection against colds, catarrh, consumption, neuralgia, rheumatism and malaria.

4th. They cannot crock, fade or poison the skin, as they are *natural colors* and contain no dyes.

5th. The Camel's Hair is warranted to wash without shrinking.

Manufactured in all styles of Gentlemen's, Ladies' and Children's Underwear and Night Shirts.

FOR SALE BY LEADING MERCHANTS.

Catalogue with Prices sent on application.

WARNER BROS., 359 Broadway, N. Y.

WILD GOAT

WHITE

RUGS

(From North China.)
36 x 68 Inches Delivered
to any part of the UNITED STATES
FREE OF CHARGE on receipt of $4,25
A.A. VANTINE & CO. 879 Broadway.

SNOW'S
Traveler's Cap and Head-Rest Combined.

THE combination of a PILLOW within a TRAVELER'S CAP is a decided novelty, and something that cannot fail to be appreciated. Although to external appearances like other silk caps, it has concealed within its lining an air cushion, which may be inflated at will, thus forming a soft head-rest which enables one to lean comfortably against any hard substance. The pad, when exhausted of air, adds but a trifle to the bulk of the cap. **Give them a trial, and you will never be without one when traveling.** Made of fine Black Gros Grain Silk, with Satin Lining. All sizes, **$1.50** each. Ask your Hatter for them. If not found, they will be sent by mail, postage prepaid, on receipt of price. State size cap usually worn. Address the Manufacturers,

GEORGE FROST & CO.
287 Devonshire Street, Boston.

JOHN BOYLE,
199, 201, 203, 205
Fulton St.,
N. Y. CITY.

The Largest Manufactory in the **U. S.**
"Dreadnaught" Waterproof Covers, for **Horses, Trucks, Carts, Stages,** &c., &c.
Duck in all widths, oiled and plain, for **Wagon Tops, Lap Aprons,** &c., &c.
Made of the best double and twist U. S. A. duck.
Boyle's Pat. Nose-Bags at wholesale.

THE BRADLEY

ROAD CART

Above illustration represents our **No. 4** or **Phaeton Cart.** We also make them with skeleton bodies, just the thing for jogging trotters or breaking colts. Our **No. 3½** or **Single Park Cart** is used very extensively by Gentlemen Drivers in speeding on the road or track, weighs 100 lbs., and as handsomely finished as the finest carriage.

THREE STYLES weighing from **90** to **160 lbs.** Prices from **$55** to **$80.**

☞ **First-Class** in every respect, and everybody likes them.

THE BRADLEY HANDY WAGON

THE BRADLEY HANDY SURREY

THE BRADLEY HANDY Buck Board

The Best on Wheels. Light, strong, convenient and low priced. **Handy** to get into and out of. **Handy** for single horse or pair. **Handy** for one person or more. **Handy** to load or unload. *Send for Free Circular, "How to purchase direct from the manufacturer."*

BRADLEY & CO. **SYRACUSE, N. Y.** **63 Murray St., New York.** **32 S. Market St. Boston.**

Price $2.50. **"VIGIL"** **Weight 6 lbs.**

The Only Combined

STOVE, LAMP, and LANTERN.

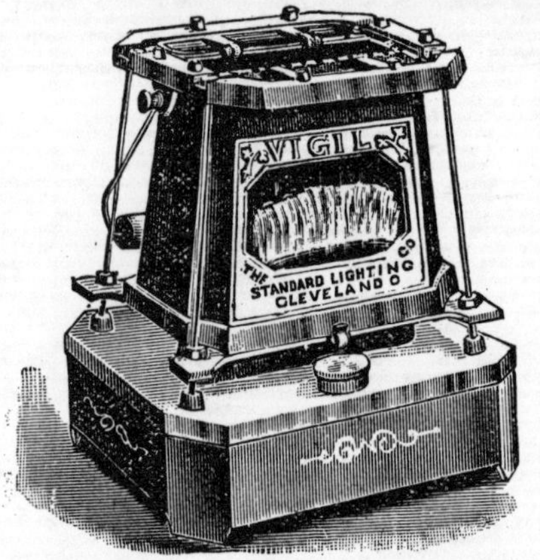

Has 4-inch Wick. Burns common Coal Oil. Handsome. Finished in Enamel and full Nickel. **Indispensable** in every family; for students, &c. Remarkable combination of *light* and *heat*. Sent to any address on receipt of price. Send for Circular.

MANUFACTURED ONLY BY

THE STANDARD LIGHTING CO.,

153 Seneca St. **Cleveland, Ohio.**

THE IMPROVED HICKOK

CALCIUM BURNER

Gives a light of sixty candle-power, equal to seven common burners, and will fit any ordinary lamp. This burner has been greatly improved, and is now beyond question the best lamp burner ever made. As a reading light it has no equal. Price, burner and chimney, $1.25.

HEKTOGRAPH MFG. CO.,

82 and 84 Church St., and 10 East Fourteenth St., N. Y.

MADAME ROWLEY'S TOILET MASK.

The following are the claims made for Madame Rowley's Toilet Mask, and the grounds on which it is recommended to ladies for Beautifying, Bleaching, and Preserving the Complexion:

FIRST—The **Mask** is **Soft** and **Flexible** in form, and can be **Easily Applied** and **Worn** without **Discomfort** or **Inconvenience.**

SECOND—It is durable, and does not dissolve or come asunder, but holds its original mask shape.

THIRD—It has been **Analyzed** by **Eminent Scientists** and **Chemical Experts,** and pronounced **Perfectly Pure** and **Harmless.**

FOURTH—With ordinary care the **Mask** will **last for years,** and its VALUABLE PROPERTIES **Never Become Impaired.**

FIFTH—The **Mask** is protected by letters-patent, and is the **only Genuine** article of the kind.

SIXTH—It is **Recommended** by **Eminent Physicians** and **Scientific Men** as a SUBSTITUTE FOR INJURIOUS COSMETICS.

THE TOILET MASK IN POSITION TO THE FACE.

SEVENTH—The **Mask** is a **Natural Beautifier,** for **Bleaching** and **Preserving** the **Skin** and **Removing Complexional Imperfections.**

COMPLEXION BLEMISHES

May be hidden imperfectly by cosmetics and powders, but can only be removed permanently by the Toilet Mask. By its use every kind of spots, impurities, roughness, etc., vanish from the skin, leaving it soft, clear, brilliant, and beautiful. It is harmless, costs little, and saves its user money. It prevents and removes wrinkles, and is both a complexion preserver and beautifier. Famous society ladies, actresses, belles, etc., use it.

THE TOILET MASK COMPANY,

Send for Descriptive Treatise. **1164 BROADWAY,** **Send for Descriptive Treatise.**

NEW YORK.

Mention this paper when you write.

DOVER EGG BEATER.

Beats the white of the Eggs *thoroughly* in 10 seconds.
The Beating floats revolve on two centres, one inch apart,
And curiously interlace each other—notice them.
"DOVER EGG BEATER" in large letters on the wheel.

Equally valuable for eggs, cake, or salad cream.
No joints or rivets to get loose. Cleaned instantly.
Money refunded if you are not delighted with it.
A woman and her "Dover Beater" cannot be separated.

The "DOVER EGG BEATER" is the only article in the wide world that is **Warranted to DELIGHT the Purchaser.** There NEVER has been, and is not now, an article made that men DARE to support with SUCH a warrant.

Dover Stamping Co., Boston, Mass., U. S. A.

THE INFALLIBLE COIN SCALE

Renders the Detection of Counterfeits Certain.

AGENTS WANTED EVERYWHERE.

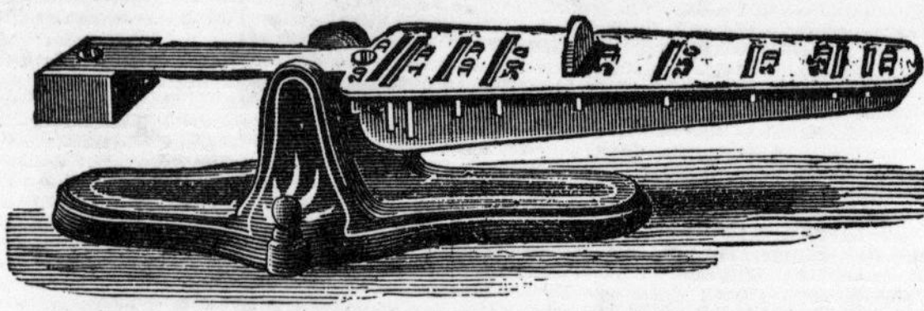

EXCLUSIVE TERRITORY GIVEN.

Used by the United States Government in all the Departments as

THE STANDARD COIN SCALE.

With each Scale we give the full standard and least current weight of all gold coins.

TREASURY OF THE UNITED STATES,
WASHINGTON, D. C., December 21, 1881.

The Detector in question has been tested at this office, and found to be accurate in the detection of all counterfeit United States gold and silver coins.
JAS. GILFILLAN, Treasurer United States.

POST OFFICE DEPARTMENT,
WASHINGTON, D. C., December 21, 1881.

I have examined the Infallible American Gold and Silver Coin Scale and Counterfeit Coin Detector carefully, and consider it accurate, durable, and cheap. THOMAS L. JAMES, Postmaster-General.

☞ **Each Scale sent in a Handsome Box, Securely Packed.**

We send with each Scale a printed guarantee for **FIVE YEARS**, and will redeem, at nominal value, all counterfeit U. S. coin that it will not detect, thus affording

ABSOLUTE INSURANCE FROM COUNTERFEITS FOR $1 A YEAR.

☞ **Sent by Registered Mail, or by Express, C. O. D., for $5.**

Insist on having one of our guarantee certificates, which we furnish with each Scale. Send Postal for testimonials. Make Money Orders or Drafts payable to order of

INFALLIBLE COIN SCALE CO., 267 Broadway, New York City.

THE AERIATRON.

The Aeriatron is a well-tried apparatus for purifying the air of sleeping-apartments, offices, crowded halls, school and Sunday-school rooms. With one charge it gives for 36 hours a continuous supply of fresh moisture to the atmosphere of a room, while, at the same time, it charges the atmosphere with any disinfectant which the water holds in solution. It thus prevents diseases which have their origin in bad air, sewer gas, and the like, while it saves us from the dry nostrils, hacking coughs, and irritated eyes which often arise from a deficient supply of pure moisture. For circulars, address Aeriatron Co., 27 East 14th St., New York.

Only Sure and Practical Protection from Flies and Mosquitoes.

Convenient—Put in or out of position in an instant.
Light—Gross weight of Frame only **Four Pounds.**
Roomy—Covers entire bed, and can be set as high as desired. Occupants can not get entangled in netting. Makes a cool and pleasant cover, as netting is stretched by frame, giving free circulation of air.
Durable—No intricate mechanism to get out of order; **plain self-acting open and shut; Strong.**
If you have a Canopy, get one of these frames and use your netting, the **Solid Comfort** received will pay you 10 times over.

BAKER'S FOLDING

AUTOMATIC BED CANOPY

When not in use, folded clear out of way against head-board, and so mosquitoes can not get under netting. When in use, netting can be tucked under bed clothing at lower edge, affording absolute protection.

Only Canopy which attaches to bed, allowing bed to be moved to any part of room. No damage to bed as it is attached below mattress.

GIVES UNDISTURBED REST TO THE SICK.

Netting can be removed for cleaning without disturbing frame. Can be ornamented with ribbons, etc., to taste.

PRICE: Frame, ready for netting, $4.00.
Give width of bed in ordering.

Two pieces of ordinary mosquito bar will make a Canopy, and can be purchased at any store, cheap, and be put on by anyone—directions sent with frame. To those wishing an extra fine netting, which is the most satisfactory and economical, we furnish a **Fine Bobinet, Round Mesh Netting, for $5.00.**

Shipped to any part of world on receipt of price. Remit by New York Draft, Registered Letter, or Postal Note. Folded compact and very light weight secure minimum express rates. Send 2c. stamp for Illustrated Circular. Special rates on large orders.
Foreign orders must make provision for transportation.

AGENTS WANTED. **A. R. BAKER, Manufacturer, INDIANAPOLIS, INDIANA, U.S.A.**

THE AUTOPHONE.

THE FINEST
AUTOMATIC MUSICAL INSTRUMENT
EVER OFFERED.

Just the thing for the Holidays.

Send for Circular and Catalogue of Music.

Address **THE AUTOPHONE CO.,**
ITHACA N. Y.

J. C. SCHNOTER'S

Patent Corset Shoulder Brace

For Round Shoulders, Narrow Chests, and Curvature of the Spine. Makes the form graceful, expands the chest, strengthens the lungs, and relieves pain and weakness in the back. Also all other kinds of Shoulder Braces. A full assortment of **TRUSSES** (Hard Rubber,

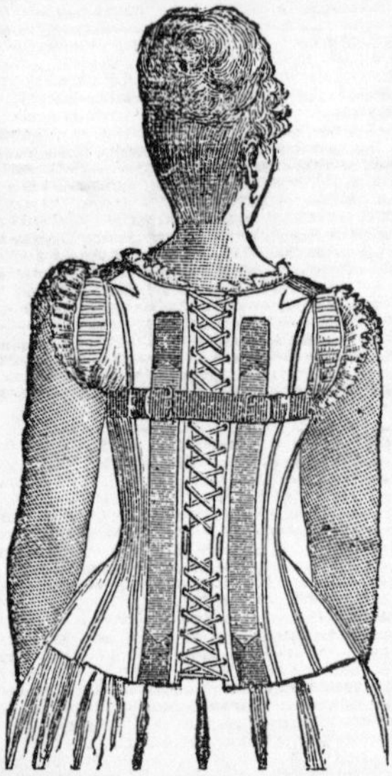

Silk and Cotton Elastic, French, and German Trusses. Elastic Stockings and Rubber **BANDAGES** for Swollen Veins, and Crutches. Also the celebrated "Schnoter's Knitted (Suspensory Bandages,)" which are sold by all Druggists in the United States.

ABDOMINAL SUPPORTERS.

"43 W. 32d St., Dec. 21st, 1872.

For some years Mr. Schnoter has made Abdominal Supporters for my female patients, and there has always been shown much able skill and judgment in their construction and adjustment. Indeed, no one else has given satisfaction so universally.

FRANK HAMILTON, M.D., LL.D., Professor of Surgery in Bellevue Hospital Medical College; Surgeon to Bellevue Hospital and to St. Francis Hosp'l, N.Y.City."

"42 W. 25th Street.

I fully endorse Prof. Hamilton's recommendation of Mr. Schnoter's Abdominal Supporters.

ALFRED L. LOOMIS, M.D., Professor of Institutes and Practice of Medicine, New York University, Physician to Bellevue and Charity Hospitals, etc."

Competent ladies in attendance for ladies. Customers attended at their residences if preferred. Goods sent out of the city by mail or express. J. C. SCHNOTER, **523 and 525 Sixth Avenue,** between 31st and 32d Streets, New York.

NEW STEEL HORSE SHOE,

With Level Spring Platform—Continuous Calk. The best in the world. Cures Tender and Contracted Feet, Corns, Interfering, Quarter-crack Lameness, and all evils resulting from the use of the common shoe. Responsible men can make money selling this Shoe. Send for pamphlet. Trial set with nails, $1.00. To measure, place foot on paper, and draw pencil around.

The JOHN D. BILLINGS PATENT HORSE SHOE COMPANY
265 Broadway, New York.

JEWETT'S REFRIGERATORS

THE PATENT

LABRADOR.

Send for Book of Information.

THE JOHN C. JEWETT MFG. CO., Buffalo, N. Y.

FACIAL BLEMISHES.

the Largest Establishment in the World for their Treatment. Facial Development, Hair and Scalp, Superfluous Hair, Birth Marks, Moles, Warts, Moth, Freckles, Wrinkles, Red Nose, Acne, Pimples, Bl'k Heads, Scars, Pitting, etc., and their treatment. Send 10c. for book of 50 pages, 4th edition.

Dr. JOHN H. WOODBURY,
87 North Pearl St., Albany, N. Y.
Established 1870. Inventor of Facial Appliances, Springs, etc. Six Parlors.

HILL'S MANUAL, by Thos. E. Hill, the original form book, though sold in the past few years from Maine to California, has been introduced only sufficiently to make the demand still greater.

In its wide range of subjects treated, including Penmanship, Primary Education, Etiquette, Social, Legal and Commercial Forms, Parliamentary Rules, etc., it appeals to the wants of all classes, and hence the growing demand for it.

TESTIMONIAL.

Prof. Geo. Soule, Pres. Soule's Com. College, New Orleans, says: "I regard Hill's Manual the most valuable book for all classes which the nineteenth century has produced."

Ex-President Grant, Senators, Governors and notables in all parts of the world have been its purchasers. Agents wanted by

The snob that presents two fingers.

The cold, lifeless hand.

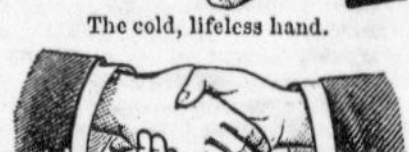

The whole-souled, hearty grasp.

Hand-Shaking

As a Form of Salutation. See Hill's Manual.

HILL STANDARD BOOK CO., 103 State Street, Chicago, Ill.

☞ Ask any Book Agent to show you Hill's Manual. ☜

From American publications of 1898.

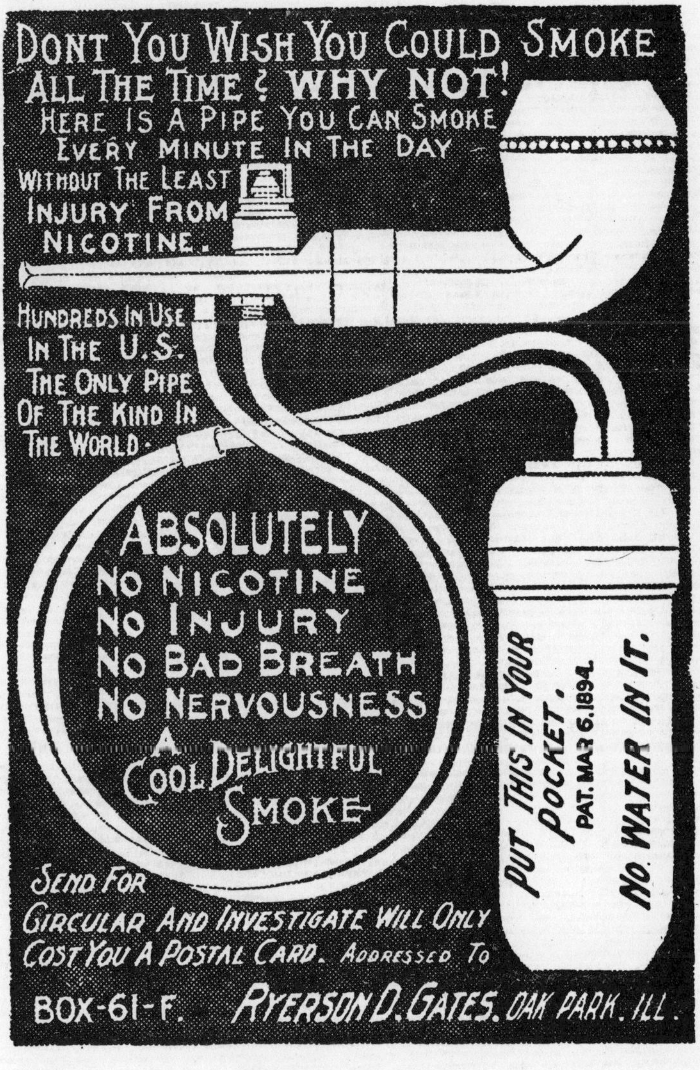

Curious and Eccentric Ads

In 1655 an English astrologer named Lilly ran this denial in the "Perfect Diurnal." Eleven years later the prediction came true in the exact areas mentioned in the ad.

An Advertisement from Mr William Lilly.

WHEREAS there are several flying reports, and many false and scandalous speeches in the mouth of many people in this City, tending unto this effect, viz. : That I, William Lilly, should predict or say there would be a great Fire in or near the Old Exchange, and another in St John's Street, and another in the Strand near Temple Bar, and in several other parts of the City. These are to certifie the whole City that I protest before Almighty God, that I never wrote any such thing, I never spoke any such word, or ever thought of any such thing, or any or all of those particular Places or Streets, or any other parts. These untruths are forged by ungodly men and women to disturb the quiet people of this City, to amaze the Nation, and to cast aspersions and scandals on me : God defend this City and all her inhabitants, not only from Fire, but from the Plague, Pestilence, or Famine, or any other accident or mortality that may be prejudicial unto her greatnesse.

A public feud between two manufacturers began in March, 1707, and went on for weeks. The following ads are from the English publication "Daily Courant."

BY John Yarwell and Ralph Sterrop, Right Spectacles, reading and other optic glasses, etc., were first brought to perfection by our own proper art, and needed not the boasted industry of our two apprentices to recommend them to the world ; who by fraudently appropriating to themselves what they never did, and obstinately pretending to what they never can perform, can have no other end in view than to astonish the ignorant, impose on the credulous, and amuse the public. For which reason and at the request of several gentlemen already imposed on, as also to prevent such further abuses as may arise from the repeated advertisements of these two wonderful performers, we John Yarwell and Ralph Sterrop do give public notice, that to any person who shall think it worth his while to make the experiment, we will demonstrate in a minute's time the insufficiency of the instrument and the vanity of the workmen by comparing their miraculous Two-Foot, with our Three and Four Foot Telescopes. And therefore, till such a telescope be made, as shall come up to the character of these unparalleled performers, we must declare it to be a very impossible thing.

WHEREAS Mr Yarwell, Mr Sterrop, and Mr Marshall, the 2 first were our Masters with whom we served our Apprenticeships, and since for several years we have made the best of work for them and Mr Marshall. And now they being envious at our prosperity have published several false, deceitful and malicious advertisements, wherein they assert that we cheat all that buy any of our goods, and that we pretend to many impossibilities, and impose on the public, they having wrested the words and sense of our advertisements, pretend that we affirm that a 2 Foot Telescope of our making will do as much as the best 4 Foot of another man's make, and they fraudulently show in their shops one of their best 4 Foots against our small one, and then cry out against the insufficiency of our instrument. Now we G. Willdey and Th. Brandreth being notoriously abused, declare that we never did assert any such thing, or ever did pretend to impossibilities, but will make good in every particular all those [note, these are their own words] (impossible, incredable, miraculous, wonderful, and astonishing) things mentioned in our advertisements; which things perhaps may be impossible, incredible, miraculous, wonderful, and astonishing to them, but we assure them they are not so to us: For we have small miraculous telescopes, as they are pleased to call them, that do such wonders that they say it is impossible to make such, by the assistance of which we will lay any person £10. that instead of 2 miles mentioned, we will tell them the hour of the day 3 if not 4 miles by such a dial as St James's or Bow.

Ads similar to these were continued by both companies until the end of May, when Willdey and Brandreth inserted this attempt to demolish their late employers. Whether the game was too expensive, or whether the old firm was shut up by this, we don't know, but it ended the contest.

We do affirm it [the telescope made by W. & B.] to be the pleasantest and usefullest instrument of this kind, and what our adversaries have said against it is false and proceeds from an ill design; we have already offered to lay them 20 guineas to their 10 that they could not make a better, but they knowing they were not capable to engage us in that particular, said in their answer that there needs no more than to compare one instrument with another that they may have the opportunity of shewing that theirs exceeds; to which proposal we do agree, and to that purpose have bought 3 of their best telescopes that we might be sure of one that was good, though they say in their advertisements that they make none but the best, and we are ready to give our oaths that no damage has been done them since they were bought. And now to bring these matters to an end, we will lay them 20 guineas to their 10, that 3 of our best of the same sizes are better than them; and any gentleman that will may see the experiment tried in an instant at our shop, where they may also see that our best pocket telescope comes not far short of their best large 4 Foot one. And several other curiosities all made to the greatest perfection. And whereas Mr Yarwell, Mr Sterrop, and Mr Marshall have maliciously, falsly, and unjustly insinuated that we are but indifferent workmen, several persons being justly moved by that scandalous aspersion, have offered to give their oaths that they have often heard them say that we were the best of workmen, and that we understood our business as well as themselves. And as such we do each of us challenge them all 3 severally to work with them, who does most and best for £20. As for the Microscope it is our own invention, and 2 of them were made by us before any person saw them, as we can prove by witnesses; as we also can their railing and scandalous aspersions to be false. All persons may be assured that all our instruments do and will answer the character given them in the advertisements of T. Brandreth and G. Willdey, &c. &c.

In the "Morning Post" of April 18, 1780 we find this ad for a hideaway for pregnant women.

ANY Lady whose Situation may require a Temporary Retirement, may be accommodated agreeable to her wishes in the house of a Gentleman of eminence in the Profession, where honour and secrecy may be depended on, and where every vestige of Pregnancy is obliterated; or any Lady who wishes to become Pregnant may have the causes of sterility removed in the safest manner. Letters (Post-paid) addressed to A. B. No. 23, Fleet Street, will be attended to.

The following is one of the earliest known newspaper advertisements, from the Dutch publication "Tydinghen" June 2, 1635. It is also the first ad known to be inserted from a foreign country.

> Licentiate Grim, British preacher and professor at the University of Wesel, has published an extensive treatise against all popish scribblers, entitled "Papal Sanctimony," that is, catholic and authentic proof that Pope John VIII., commonly called Pope Jutte [Joan], was a woman.

This example of combining business with mourning, in the form of an advertising tombstone, is said to have stood in the churchyard cemetery in Gateshead, England in the early 1800's.

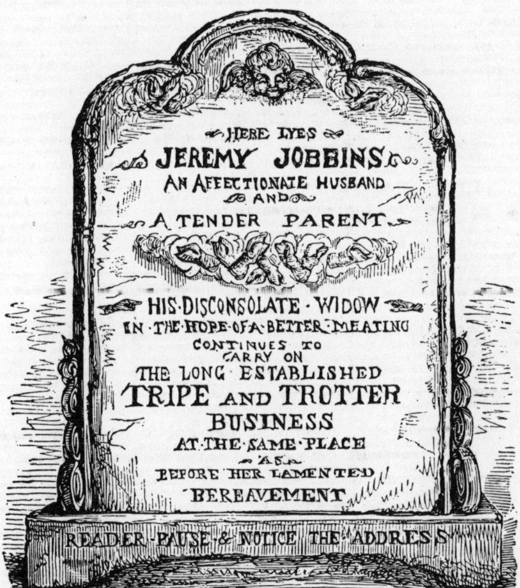

Another example of mixing mourning with money making is illustrated in the following notice from a Spanish newspaper.

> This morning our Saviour summoned away the jeweller, Siebald Illmaga, from his shop to another and a better world. The undersigned, his widow, will weep upon his tomb, as will also his two daughters, Hilda and Emma; the former of whom is married, and the latter is open to an offer. The funeral will take place to-morrow. —His disconsolate widow, Veronique Illmaga. P.S. This bereavement will not interrupt our employment which will be carried on as usual, only our place of business will be removed from No. 3, Tessi de Teinturiers to No. 4, Rue de Missionaire, as our grasping landlord has raised our rent.

From the "British Chronicle," January 20, 1762.

> This day was published, price 1s.,
>
> SOME authentic particulars of the life of John Macnaghton, Esq., of Ben ——, who was executed in Ireland, on tuesday the 25th day of December, for the Murder of Miss Mary Anne Knox, the only daughter of Andrew Knox, Esq., of Prehen, representative in the late and present Parliament for the county of Donegal. With a full account of his pretended Connexion with the young Lady; of the measures he took to seize her person previous to the Murder; the circumstances of that fact; the manner of his being apprehended; and his conduct and behaviour from that time till his Death. Compiled from papers communicated by a gentleman in Ireland, to a person of distinction of that Kingdom now residing here.
>
> Printed for H. Payne & W. Croply, at Dryden's Head in Paternoster Row.

From the English newspaper "Daily Advertiser," of July 1776.

> TWO Men beg leave to acquaint the Public in general that they keep the cleanest Barber's Shop in all London, where the people can have their Hair cut for 2d., dressed for 3d., and be shaved for 1d. One of these Men can bleed and draw teeth very well; he bleeds both in the English and German manner, as well at home as abroad, and is exceeding careful. Bleeding 3d., drawing teeth 4d. There is a parlour made in the shop on purpose for bleeding and drawing teeth. The people may depend on being served immediately and well in every respect. No satisfaction, no pay. The above-mentioned Shop is at No. 7 King Street, Seven Dials.

A 1699 English handbill.

That Prodigy in Nature,

By His Majeſty's Authority.

At the Sign of *Charing-Croſs*, at *Charing-Croſs*.

THere is to be ſeen a ſtrange and monſtrous Child, with one Body, and one Belly, and yet otherwiſe it hath all the Proporſions of two Children, that is two Heads, two Noſes, two Mouths, four Eyes, four Ears, four Arms, and four Leggs, four Hands, and four Feet, the monſter is of the femal kind, it was born at Fillips Town on the Twenty Ninth of April, 1699 The Father of this monſter is preſent where it is to be ſeen.

From the "London Daily Post and General Advertiser," March 15, 1740.

MARY SOUTHALL

Successor to John Southall, *the first and only person that ever found out the nature of* BUGGS, *Author of the Treatise of those nauseous venomous Insects, published with the Approbation (and for which he had the honour to receive the unanimous Thanks) of the Royal Society,*

GIVES NOTICE,

THAT since his decease she hath followed the same business, and lives at the house of Mrs Mary Roundhall, in Bearlane, Christ Church Parish, Southwark. Such quality and gentry as are troubled with buggs, and are desirous to be kept free from those vermin, may know, on sending their commands to her lodgings aforesaid, when she will agree with them on easy terms, and at the first sight will justly tell them which of their beds are infested, &c., and which are free, and what is the expense of clearing the infested ones, never putting any one to more expense than necessary.

Persons who cannot afford to pay her price, and is willing to destroy them themselves, may by sending notice to her place of abode aforesaid, be furnish'd with the NON PAREIL LIQUOR, &c. &c.

From "Faulkner's Dublin Journal," February 1762.

WHEREAS a lady who called herself a native of Ireland was in England in the year 1740, and resided some time at a certain village near Bath, where she was delivered of a son, whom she left with a sum of money under the care of a person in the same parish, and promised to fetch him at a certain age, but has not since been heard of; now this is to desire the lady, if living, and this should be so fortunate as to be seen by her, to send a letter, directed to T. E. to be left at the Chapter Coffee house, St Paul's Churchyard, London, wherein she is desired to give an account of herself, and her reasons for concealing this affair: or if the lady should be dead, and any person is privy to the affair, they are likewise desired to direct as above.—*N.B.* This advertisement is published by the person himself, not from motives of necessity, or to court any assistance (he being, by a series of happy circumstances, possessed of an easy and independent fortune) but with a real desire to know his origin.—*P.S.* The strictest secrecy may be depended on.

The following are wedding invitations that were published in the English newspaper "Cumberland Pacquet," and are quite typical of the period. The first is from 1786, the second from 1836.

INVITATION.

Suspend for one day your cares and your labours,
And come to this wedding, kind friends and good neighbours.

NOTICE is hereby given that the marriage of ISAAC PEARSON with FRANCES ATKINSON will be solemnized in due form in the parish church of Lamplugh, in Cumberland, on Tuesday next, the 30th of May inst.; immediately after which the bride and bridegroom with their attendants will proceed to Lonefoot, in the said parish, where the nuptials will be celebrated by a variety of rural entertainments.

Then come one and all
At Hymen's soft call
From Whitehaven, Workington, Harrington, Dean,
Hail, Ponsonby, Blaing and all places between,
From Egremont, Cockermouth, Barton, St Bee's,
Cint, Kinnyside, Calder and parts such as these;
And the country at large may flock in if they please.
Such sports there will be as have seldom been seen,
Such wrestling, and fencing and dancing between,
And races for prizes, for frolick and fun,
By horses, and asses, and dogs will be run
That you'll all go home happy—as sure as a gun.
In a word, such a wedding can ne'er fail please;
For the sports of Olympus were trifles to these.

Nota Bene.—You'll please to observe that the day
Of this grand bridal pomp is the thirtieth of May,
When 'tis hop'd that the sun, to enliven the sight,
Like the flambeau of Hymen, will deign to burn bright.

CARMARTHEN, April 12, 1836.

AS we intend to enter the MATRIMONIAL STATE on THURSDAY, the 5th of MAY next, we are encouraged by our Friends to make a BIDDING on the occasion the same Day, at the Sign of the ANGEL, situate in LAMMAS-STREET; when and where the favour of your good and agreeable Company is most humbly solicited, and whatever donation you may be pleased to confer on us then, will be thankfully received, warmly acknowledged, and cheerfully repaid whenever called for on a similar occasion,

By your most obedient humble Servants,

DAVID DANIEL
(Shoemaker,)
RUTH EVANS.

From a daily paper of Calcutta in 1818.

FEMALES RAFFLED FOR.—Be it known, that Six Fair Pretty Young LADIES, with two sweet and engaging CHILDREN, lately imported from Europe, having roses of health blooming on their cheeks, and joy sparkling in their eyes, possessing amiable tempers and highly accomplished, whom the most indifferent cannot behold without expressions of rapture, are to be raffled for, next door to the British Gallery. Scheme: Twelve Tickets, at 12 rupees each; the highest of the three throws, doubtless, takes the most fascinating, &c. &c.

From American newspapers of the 1880's.

LEGS AND ARMS
(ARTIFICIAL)
WITH RUBBER FEET AND HANDS.

Indorsed by the U.S. Government, the Most Eminent Surgeons in the Country, the Press, and over 8000 Men, Women, and Children who wear them residing in all parts of the World.

The Rubber Foot and Hand possess the most natural appearance, the greatest durability, and the greatest degree of comfort of all artificial limbs. Vast numbers of mutilated men and women are, by the use of rubber feet and hands, enabled to mingle with the rest of the world without betraying their loss or experiencing great inconvenience.

The accompanying engraving represents a sailor of the late rebellion who lost his leg and arm by the explosion of a shell in a naval combat. He has been practically restored to his usefulness by the application of Marks' Patent Artificial Limbs with rubber hands and feet. Large illustrated pamphlet containing over 300 testimonials and copyright formula for taking measurement sent free.

A. A. MARKS, 701 Broadway, New York City.

From a New York paper in 1822.

ANY person in want of a DEAD PIG may find one, that will probably answer his purpose, in the middle of Broadway, between Broome and Spring Streets. Applicants need not be in any great haste, as it is expected that he will lie there several days; and if the warm weather should last, and the carriages will let him alone, he will grow *—bigger and bigger.*

Of all the flowery advertisements ever written, this ad for land on the Hudson River has to take all time saccharine sweet award.

I can sell for eighteen hundred and thirty nine dollars, a palace, a sweet and pensive retirement, on the virgin banks of the Hudson, containing 85 acres. The land is luxuriously divided by the hand of nature and art, into pasture and tillage, into plain and declivity, into the stern abruptness and the dalliance of most tufted meadow. Streams of sparkling gladness (thick with trout) dance through this wilderness of beauty, to the music of the cricket and grasshopper. The evergreen sighs as the evening zephyr flits through its shadowy bosom, and the aspen trembles like the love-splitting heart of a damsel. Fruits of the tropics in golden beauty melt on the bows, and the bees go heavy and sweet from the fields to their garnering hives. The stables are worthy of the steeds of Nimrod or the studs of Achilles, and its henery was built expressly for the birds of paradise; while sombre in the distance, like the cave of a hermit, glimpses are caught of the dog house. Here poets have come and warbled their lays, here sculptors have cut, here painters have robbed the scene of dreamy landscapes, and here the philosopher discovered the stone which made him the alchymist of nature. As the young moon hangs like a cutting of silver from the blue breast of the sky, an angel may be seen each night dancing with golden tiptoes on the greensward. (N.B. This angel goes with the place.)

From an 1855 edition of the "London Times."

IT WOULD BE A NOBLE ACT OF HUMANITY if any generous and kind-hearted individual would procure or grant EMPLOYMENT to a suffering individual, in whose behalf this appeal is made. He is of high rank, education, and manners, and in every point of view fit to fill any situation. He is without influential friends, and from complicated frauds and misfortunes, is unable to continue the education of eight lovely children. He seeks nothing for himself, except to be so placed, giving to the hands of his kind benefactor all he receives for his children's present and future support. This will save him from a broken heart. Any situation that will enable him to effect this object will be received with heartfelt gratitude, and filled with honour, assiduity, and fidelity. Most respectable reference, &c. N.B. No pecuniary assistance can be received. Address ——.

From "Harpers Weekly" in 1887

A SCRAP-BOOK
FOR
"HOMELY WOMEN" ONLY.

We dedicate this collection of toilet secrets, not to the pretty women (they have advantages enough, without being told how to double their beauty), but to the plainer sisterhood, to those who look in the glass and are not satisfied with what they see. To such we bring abundant help.

CONTENTS. Part 1—Part 2.

Practical devices for ugly ears, mouths, fingertips, crooked teeth.
To reduce flesh, etc.
How to bleach and refine a poor skin.
Freckles, Pimples, Moles, etc.
Mask of Diana of Poictiers.
Out of 100 Cosmetics, which to choose.
How to make and apply them for daylight, evening, and the stage (one saves two thirds, and has a better article by making instead of buying Cosmetics).
What goes to constitute a belle.
Madame Vestris's methods for private Theatricals. How to sit for a photograph successfully, and other toilet hints.

Send $1.00, a two-cent stamp, and an envelope addressed to yourself.

BROWN, SHERBROOK, & CO.,
27 Hollis Street, Boston, Mass.

The following editorial advertisement was published by an Illinois journalist, on assuming the duties of chief of the staff in the mid 1800's.

Sensational, distressing details of revolting murders and shocking suicides respectfully solicited. Bible class presentations and ministerial donation parties will be "done" with promptness and despatch. Keno banks and their operations made a speciality. Accurate reports of Sunday School anniversaries guaranteed. The local editor will cheerfully walk 17 miles after Sunday school to see and report a prize fight. Funerals and all other melancholy occasions written up in a manner to challenge admiration. Horse races reported in the highest style of the reportorial art. Domestic broils and conjugal felicities sought for with untiring avidity. Police court proceedings and sermons reported in a manner well calculated to astonish the prisoner, magistrate, and preacher.

At this same time the "San Francisco Newsletter" had an unusual way of dealing with companies that refused to advertise in its pages. This is one example of the paper's animosity towards a reluctant advertiser.

A PERMANENT PARAGRAPHIC ADVERTISEMENT.

[RESPECTFULLY DEDICATED TO THE SPRING VALLEY WATER WORKS.]

A miner's inch of water is about twenty thousand gallons. The usual price for an inch of water in the mines is ten cents. The Spring Valley Company sells water in large quantities at seventy-five cents per thousand gallons, or at fifteen dollars seventy-five cents per inch—which is one hundred and fifty-seven times the price which miners pay. Furnished in small quantities to housekeepers, the Company charges from thirty to fifty dollars an inch—five hundred times the miners' rates.

IGNOTUS.

From American newspapers of the 1880's.

COMIC CARDS, 12 cents a Set.

"I'm Engaged," 5 Awful Funny. "I'm a Daddy," 5 " " "Yachtsman and Scullers," 6 very Comic. "Monkeys," 6 Holiday Celebrations. "Too Too," Minds *vs.* Dinner, 4 Comic. "Comic Billiard Players," etc., 4 Comic. "Tommy" Cat's Night Out, 6 very Funny. "Girls with Pets," 4 very elegant. "Comic Man," moves Eyes and Tongue. "De Æsthetic Nigger," Large Colored, 20c. "Broke your Back Mania," " 20c.

Entire lot for $1.00. *Agents wanted.*

HAPPY HOURS BAZAR, 21 Beekman Street, N. Y.

In 1826 this request for a minister was published in the "Monthly Mirror."

WANTED, for a newly erected Chapel, near Grosvenor Square, a gentleman of elegant manners, and insinuating address, to conduct the theological department to a refined audience. It is not necessary that he believe in the Thirty-nine Articles ; but it is expected that he should possess a white hand and a diamond ring; he will be expected to leave out vulgar ideas, and denunciations against polite vices which he may meet with in the Bible; and, upon no account, be guilty of wounding the ears of his auditory with the words h—ll, or d——n. One who lisps, is near-sighted, and who has a due regard for amiable weaknesses, will be preferred.

N.B.—If he is of pleasing and *accommodating* manners, he will have a chance of being introduced to the first company, and three card parties every Sunday evening. One who knows a few college jokes, or who has been Chaplain to the Whip Club, will be preferred. He will have no occasion to administer Baptism, &c. &c. there being an old gentleman employed, who, on account of extreme distress, has agreed, for ten pounds per annum, to preach in the afternoon, and do all the under work.

Letters must be addressed to James Speculate, Esq. Surveyor's Office, New Square, Mary-le-Bone.

This ad for the appearance of an American comedian in England ran in a theatrical paper in the 1870's.

SAVED.

It was a chill November eve and on the busy town
A heavy cloud of yellow fog was sinking slowly down;
Upon the bridge of Waterloo, a prey to mad despair,
There stood a man with heavy brow and deep-lined face of care.

One ling'ring look around he gave, then on the river cast
That sullen stare of rash resolve he meant should be his last.
Far down the old cathedral rose, a shadow grey and dim,
The light of day would dawn on that but ne'er again on him.

One plunge within the murky stream would end the bitter strife.
" What rest's there now," he sobbed aloud, " to bid me cling to life?"
Just then the sound of stamping feet smote on his list'ning ear,
A sandwich-man upon his beat paused 'neath the lamplight clear.

One hurried glance—he read the board that hung upon his back,
He leapt down from the parapet, and smote his thigh a smack.
" I must see that," he cried—the words that put his woe to flight
Were "John S. Clarke as Acres at the Charing Cross to-night."

This quaint request ran in the English paper "Morning Post" on December 4, 1811.

A COOK-HOUSEMAID, or HOUSEMAID-COOK is wanted, for the service of a single gentleman, where only one other, a man-servant is kept. The age of the woman wanted must not be less than 25, nor more than 40 years; and it is requisite that she should be equally excellent in the two capacities of Cook and Housemaid. Her character must be unexceptionable for sobriety, honesty and cleanliness. The sobriety, however, which consists in drinking deep without staggering will not do; nor will the honesty suffice which would make up for the possible absence of pilfering by waste. Neither will the cleanliness answer which is content with bustling only before the employer's eyes—a sure symptom of a slattern. The servant advertised for, must be thoroughly and truly cleanly, honest and sober. As it is probable that not a drab out of place who reads this advertisement but will be for imposing herself, though, perhaps, incapable of cooking a sprat, and about as nice as a Hottentot, all such are warned not to give themselves useless trouble. On the other hand, a steady, clean woman, really answering the above description, will, by applying as below, hear of a place not easy equalled in comfort; where the wages are good and constantly increasing, and where servants are treated as fellow-creatures, and with a kindness, which, to the discredit of their class, is seldom merited. Personal application to be made, from one to three o'clock, to Mr Danvers, perfumer, No. 16, Craven Street, Strand.

From the American publication "Harpers Weekly" in the 1880's.

TELEPHONES SOLD.

Don't pay exorbitant rental fees to the Bell Telephone Monopoly to use their Telephones on lines less than two miles in length. A few months' rental buys a first-class Telephone that is no infringement, and works splendid on lines for private use on any kind of wire, and works good in stormy weather. It makes homes pleasant; annihilates time; prevents burglaries; saves many steps, and is just what every business man and farmer should have to connect stores, houses, depots, factories, colleges, etc., etc. The only practicable and reliable Telephone that is sold outright and warranted to work.

Chance for agents. No previous experience required. Circulars free. WM. L. NORTON, Buffalo, N.Y.

The following sarcastic advertisement ran in an English newspaper in 1816.

WANTED IMMEDIATELY, to enable me to leave the house which I have for these last five years inhabited, in the same plight and condition in which I found it, 500 LIVE RATS, for which I will gladly pay the sum of £5 sterling; and as I cannot leave the farm attached thereto in the same order in which I got it, without at least Five Millions of Docks, Dockens (weeds), I do hereby promise a further sum of £5 for said number of Dockens. Apply ——.

Dated, 31 October, 1816.

N.B. The Rats must be full grown, and no cripples.

From American publications of the 1880's.

THE BURGLAR COULDN'T FRIGHTEN HIM.

"No, my burglarious friend, I shall throw up nothing at all! I am under the protection of the United States Mutual Accident Association, 320 Broadway, New York. If you wound me I get $50 a week. If disabled permanently I get $2500. If you hit me in the eye I get $1300; for both eyes I get $5000; for hand or foot $5000; for both $10,000. And if you should kill me my family get $10,000, and could live in opulence for the rest of their lives. Blaze away!"

This wild handbill was distributed in London in the early 1800's.

MAY THE WINGS OF EXTRAVAGANCE *be clipped by the Scissars of Economy*—was the constant toast of a person who knew very well the value of a sixpence. To all good economists would Romanis wish to be recommended, though but a bad practitioner himself, (he is a little like the clergy—"Don't do as I do, but as I tell you to do.") When you want real good Stockings at a low price, come to the Sign of the Regent, 33 in Cheapside—there you have them in perfection, and I am certain sixpence in a pair is worth saving; and any one that is possest of the least spark of parsimony will give their assent. Frugality is certainly a good thing—it enables a people to pay taxes—to pay their armies—to thrash the French—to make peace on good terms—to extend commerce—to make people live long and comfortable:

FOR STOCKINGS

Romanis against the whole World, at his Mart, 33 Cheapside.

This ad ran in a tribune of February 1861, and was probably one of the first attempts at making a profit from the Civil War.

IMPORTANT FROM CHARLESTOWN!

MAJOR ANDERSON TAKEN!

ENTRANCE OBTAINED UNDER A FLAG OF TRUCE!

NEW YORKERS IMPLICATED!

GREAT EXCITEMENT! WHAT WILL THE SOUTHERN CONFEDERACY DO NEXT?

ON the 8th instant, about twelve hours before midnight, under cover of a bright sun, Col. George S. Cooke, of the Charlestown Photographic *Light* Artillery, with a strong force, made his way to Fort Sumter. On being discovered by the vigilant sentry, he ran up a flag of truce. The gate of the fortress being open, Col. Cooke immediately and heroically penetrated to the presence of Major Anderson, and levelling a double barrelled camera, demanded his unconditional surrender in the name of E. Anthony and the Photographic Community. Seeing that resistance would be in vain, the Major at once surrendered, and was borne in triumph to Charlestown, forwarded to New York, and is now on sale in the shape of Exquisite Card Photographs at 28 cents per copy, by E. Anthony, &c. &c.

This purely unselfish promise ran in the "New York Sun" in 1870's.

TRIED friends the best of friends. Since the suspension of H. C. Thorpe's advertisements, the number of deaths by consumption is truly astonishing; advertisements will now appear for the benefit of the afflicted.

American/Chinese handbill of the mid 1800's.

記隆泰祥

Chong thie Loong kee.

Most humbly beg leave to acqu :aint the Gentlemen trading to this kort that the above mention :ed chop has been long established dnd is much esteemed for its Black and young Hyson Tea but fearing the foreigners might be cheated by tho :se shumeless persons who forged this chop he therefore take the liberty to pallish these few lines for its remark and trust.

The Quack Electric Craze

Beginning in the late 1870's, the magic selling word was "Electric." Very few people even had electricity at this time, but this was of little importance because the products actually had nothing to do with electrical power as we know it. They were simply magnetized and given a quick electrical jolt at the factory.

Dr. Scott seems to have been the leader of the electrical product salesmen. He was one of the biggest advertisers of his day, purchasing large ads in American, European and Canadian periodicals. According to the doctor, "Electricity is the steam in the human engine which keeps it going and regulates its movements. It is the Vital Spark, life itself, providing all nature with the power to kill and cure."

DR. SCOTT'S
ELECTRIC CURATIVE
APPLIANCES.

Hair Brushes, Cure Headache in five minutes	$3.00
Flesh Brush, Cures Rheumatism and aches .	3.00
Horse Brush, Cures Lameness and Stiffness .	5.00
Tooth Brush, Bristles do not come out	.50
Corsets, Prevent and Cure Sickness, $1, $1.50, $2,	3.00
Corset, Nursing	1.50
Corsets, Abdominal, 18 to 36 inches	3.00
Hair Curler, Curls, Bangs and Crimps	.50
Nerve and Lung Invigorator 100 Magnet Power	10.00
" " " 50 " " .	5.00
Gentlemen's Belt, Adjustable, Full Power . .	3.00
Ladies' Abdominal Supporter	12.00
Ladies' Belt, Adjustable, Full Power	3.00
Sleeping Caps, all sizes, 30 Magnet Power . .	3.00
Office Cap (Silk), all sizes, 25 Magnet Power .	3.00
Sciatic Appliance, all sizes	8.00
Leg Appliance, all sizes	5.00
Shoulder Appliance, all sizes	5.00
Knee Cap, all sizes	5.00
Suspensory, Complete (Fine Silk)	5.00
Chest Protector	3.00
Anklet, each, all sizes	3.00
Wristlet, each, all sizes	2.50
Throat Protector, all sizes, Prevents Pneumonia	3.00
Insoles, per pair, all sizes, Prevent Cold Feet	.50
Teething Necklace, Helps the Little Ones . .	.50

MAILED FREE, $6.

ELECTROPATHIC ASSOCIATION
BELT OF LIFE.

Only Address in New York, 12 East Fourteenth Street.

MAILED FREE, $6.

ELECTRICITY, NATURE'S OWN REMEDY, AND CHIEF RESTORER OF IMPAIRED VITAL ENERGY.

Professor Baker's Belt of Life.

The only effectual, rational and simple adaptation of Self-Applicable Medical Electricity for the treatment of Rheumatism, Gout, Neuralgia, Deafness, Paralysis, Sciatica, Lumbago, Indigestion, Epilepsy, Nervous or General Debility, and other Nervous, Muscular and Functional Derangements.

On receipt of post-office order, draft or currency, for $6, payable to G. J. BAKER, Managing Director, THE ELECTROPATHIC ASSOCIATION, LIMITED, 12 East 14th St., N. Y., with measurement round waist under all clothing, we will forward free, to any part of the United States, the BELT OF LIFE as represented in the picture. Reference, our bankers, Messrs. Brown Bros. & Co., 59 Wall Street, N. Y.

Belts of Higher Power, $12 and $18.

GALVANIC GENERATOR

WHEN WORN LIKE A PAD,

QUICKLY RELIEVES

Stomach, Liver and Kidney Complaints, Rheumatism, Neuralgia, Dyspepsia, Constipation, Lumbago, Sciatica, Aches and Pains, Heartburn, Flatulency, Gout, Nervous Troubles, Weak Stomach, Debility, Weak Back, Vertigo, Indigestion, and all their Complications.

THERE IS NO WAITING. IT ACTS IMMEDIATELY.

A Guarantee goes with every Generator, our Motto being "No Cure, no pay."

The Pall Mall Electric Assoc'n

OF LONDON.

New York Branch, 842 Broadway.

We will send it

POSTPAID ON RECEIPT OF $1;

(*Mention this paper.*) Or by Express, C.O.D., at your expense, with privilege of opening and examining.

MONEY RETURNED IF NOT AS REPRESENTED.

Remittances should be made payable to

GEO. A. SCOTT 842 Broadway, New York.

They can be made in checks, drafts, post-office orders or currency. Liberal discount to druggists.

(*AGENTS WANTED IN EVERY TOWN.*)

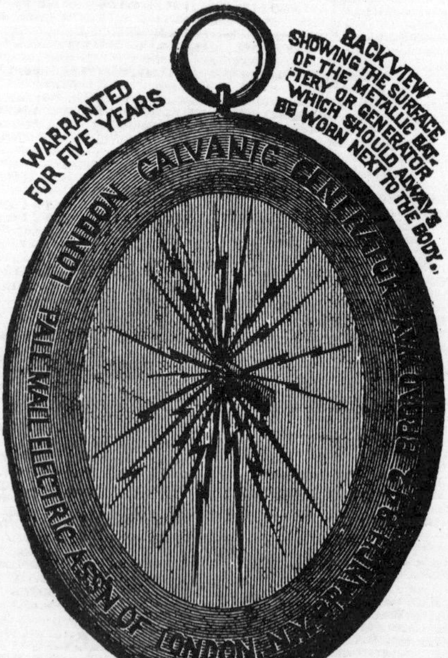

DR. SCOTT'S ELECTRIC TOOTH BRUSH.
A Remarkable Invention!!
Great Annoyance has been caused to all people using Tooth Brushes by the bristles coming out in the mouth. The Pall Mall Electric Association of London now take pleasure in introducing to the American public a Tooth Brush which they guarantee free from this troublesome defect, common to all other Tooth Brushes. The bristles are inserted in the handle by a patented process, which renders it simply impossible for them to come out in use. They are
WARRANTED THE MOST DURABLE IN THE WORLD.
In addition to this, the handle of the Brush is made of a newly invented material permanently charged with an eletro-magnetic current, which acts, without any shock, immediately upon the nerves and tissues of the teeth and gums. The act of brushing causes this current to flow into the nerve cells and roots of the teeth, and, like water poured upon a plant, it invigorates and vitalizes every part, arresting decay, building up and restoring the natural whiteness of the enamel, and quickly imparting pearly teeth and healthful, rosy gums to all using it. The handle is strong, beautifully polished, not affected by acids, impervious to moisture, and forever free from that unpleasant, musty odor exuding from wet bone handles.
THE ROYAL DENTAL SOCIETY of ENGLAND
Testify in the strongest terms as to the quick benefits following the use of this Brush, and many experts in dentistry declare it to be the greatest invention in dental appliances since the manufacture of artificial teeth.
Readthe following:
The "DENTAL REVIEW" says:
"The Electric Tooth Brush answers a long felt want, and we are convinced that it will prevent decay, and in a rational and healthy manner quickly restore the white Natural Color of the teeth unless decay is too far advanced. We congratulate the proprietors and the public upon its introduction, and believe its sale will be almost unlimited. We understand that it has already made its way into the toilets of leading London society, and we wish it all success, as it deserves."
J. C. VARLEY, Esq., the Eminent Electrician, writes:
"GENTLEMEN: Your Electric Tooth Brush must prove a boon to humanity. In all of my connection with electricity and its effects, I have never known it likely to do direct good to so many people as in its application to your Tooth Brush. You have my full encouragement and indorsement, and henceforth no other Tooth Brush shall be used in my family."
The Bristles Cannot Come Out.
DR. SCOTT'S "ELECTRIC" LONDON
Ask for Dr. SCOTT'S.
TAKE NO OTHER.
See that NAME IS ON THE BOX AND BRUSH.
MENTION THIS PAPER.
50 CENTS EACH. POST-PAID.
It is time that a long-suffering public should know that the ordinary tooth brushes sold at 20c., 25c. and 30c. each are all defective ones or "seconds," as they are called in the trade. EVERY maker carefully sorts out these defective brushes and sells them at a low price, while his first quality retail at from 35c. to 60c. each. You may rely upon this being the invariable rule, as any honorable druggist will tell you if you ask him.
A BEAUTIFUL BRUSH We will send it on trial, post-paid, on receipt of 50 cents, which will be returned if not as represented.
Seven Brushes will be mailed for the price of six, or request your nearest druggist or fancy store to obtain one for you, and be sure Dr. Scott's name is on the Brush. MONEY RETURNED if not as Represented. As soon as you receive the Brush, if not well satisfied with your bargain, write us, and we will return the money. What can be fairer? Remittances should be made payable to GEO. A. SCOTT, 842 Broadway, New York. They can be made in Checks, Drafts, Post-office Orders, Currency, or Stamps. Agents wanted in every Town.

Health! Comfort! Elegance!

DR. SCOTT'S Electric Corset.

Positively Secured with this

BEAUTIFUL INVENTION

By a happy thought Dr. Scott, of London, the Inventor of the celebrated Electric Brushes, has adapted Electro-Magnetism to Ladies' Corsets, thus bringing this wonderful curative agency within the reach of every lady.

They should be adopted at once by those suffering from any bodily ailment, and she who wishes to

Ward Off Disease,

Preserve her good health, and retain and improve the elegance of her figure should give them an immediate trial. It has been found that **magnetic treatment** makes the muscles and tissues more plastic and yielding, and it is argued from this that **Ladies who wear these corsets will have no difficulty in moulding the figure to any desired form, without tight lacing.** A tendency to extreme fatness or leanness **is a disease** which, in most cases, these articles will be found to cure. In appearance they do not differ from the usual corsets, being made of the same materials and shape (see cut). They are worn the same, and fit the same, but give a more graceful figure.

> **The Secretary of the Pall Mall Electric Association of London "earnestly recommends all" "Ladies suffering from any" "bodily ailment to adopt" "these corsets without delay." "They perform astonishing" "cures and invigorate every" "part of the system."**

In place of the ordinary steel busks in front, and a rib or two at the back, Dr. Scott inserts steel **magnetods** which are exactly the same size, shape, length, breadth and thickness as the usual steel busk or rib. By this means he is able to bring the magnetic power into constant contact with all the vital organs, and yet preserve that symmetry and lightness so desirable in a good corset. It is affirmed by professional men that there is hardly a disease which Electricity and Magnetism will not benefit or cure.

Dr. W. A. Hammond, of New York,

Late Surgeon-General of the United States, an eminent authority, publishes almost miraculous cures made by him, and all medical-men-daily practice the same. Ask your own physician. The sale of Magnetic Clothing, Band, Belts, etc., has attained world-wide success, but many who are constrained to use them are deterred because they are either expensive, bulky, troublesome, or interfere with the dress and figure. The cut gives a fair representation of the corset, which should be worn daily in place of the ordinary one, and will always do good, never harm. There is no shock or sensation whatever felt in wearing them, while benefit quickly foll ws. Being made with better material and workmanship than any corset sold, they will outwear three of those commonly used. In ordering **be careful to send exact waist measure, and mention this paper.** They are all of the same quality, differing only in size. The material is white, fine in texture, beautifully embroidered and trimmed.

We will send it on trial, postpaid, on receipt of $3.00, which will be returned if not as represented.

Inclose 10 cents extra and we guarantee safe delivery. We will send it by express, C.O.D., at your expense, with privil ge of examination—but expressage adds considerably to your cost. Or request your nearest Dry Goods or Fancy Store to obtain one for you, and be sure Dr. Scott's name is on the corset. Remittances should be made payable to **GEO. A. SCOTT, 842 Broadway, New York.** They can be made in Checks, Drafts, Post Office Orders, Currency, or Stamps. LIBERAL DISCOUNT TO THE TRADE. **Agents Wanted in every town.** Send for circular of Dr. Scott's Electric Hair Brush.

DR. SCOTT'S ELECTRIC *FLESH* BRUSH.

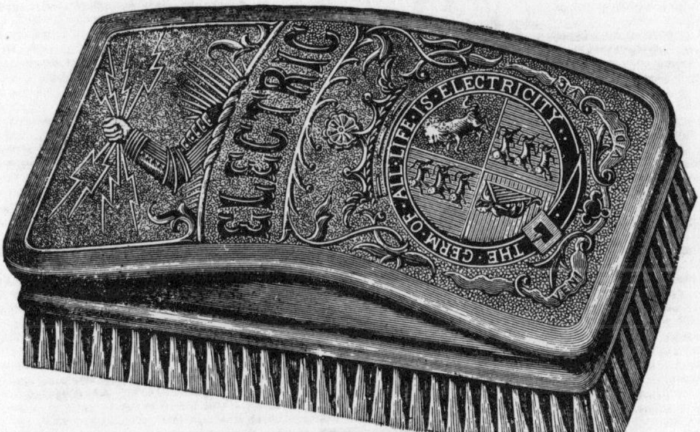

IT CURES

Rheumatism, Sciatica, Gout, Nervous Debility, Lumbago, Neuralgia, Toothache, Malarial Lameness, all Pains and Aches resulting from Colds, Impure Blood, and Impaired Circulation. It acts quickly in Stomach, Liver, and Kidney Troubles, and is a valuable assistant in their Treatment. It quickly Removes those "Back Aches" peculiar to *LADIES*.

Proprietors: The Pall Mall Electric Association of London. New York Branch: 842 Broadway.

TESTIMONIALS.

ATWOOD'S PHARMACY, Broadway, New York, May 15, 1881.

Dr. Scott: I have sold at retail over my counter, during the last few months, over $3,500 worth of your Electric Brushes at $3.00 each. They give splendid satisfaction, and many have come back and bought the second, third, and fourth one. I have heard many customers praise them highly, and from my own personal knowledge, I know of most remarkable cures attending their use. I cordially recommend them to the public." HERMON W. ATWOOD.

"I prescribe it for my patients with the happiest results. Its cures are unquestionable." DR. JOHN GAVETT GIBSON, F.C.S.

"Better than all liniments and embrocations. We cannot too highly recommend it to the afflicted." SURGICAL GAZETTE.

"For some time past I have suffered from Rheumatism in my knee, I tried your Brush and the result astonished me, in less than three minutes the pain disappeared and I have not had it since. Wishing to convince myself still further, I took it to my place of business and cured two workmen of Neuralgia and a third of Toothache. I am now satisfied with the virtue of your Brush, and do not hesitate to speak a good word for it to suffering humanity."

Yours respectfully, JESSE M. HARR.

Space forbids our publishing innumerable letters of praise and gratitude from those using our Brush. Where addresses are not given they will be furnished with pleasure on application.

Patents applied for in England, Canada, and America.

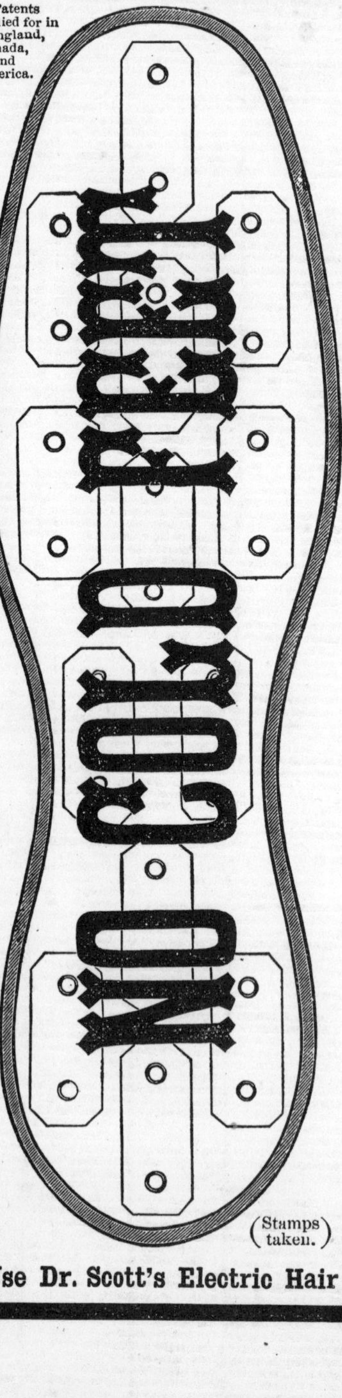

FERRIC ODYLINE,

A NEW DISCOVERY.

The Highest form of Electricity.

THOUSANDS OF PERSONS

Are now writhing in Disease, all of whom date the contraction of their different Maladies from the catching of a cold from

DAMP OR COLD FEET.

"Keep the feet warm and the head cool" is an axiom as old as the hills and yet is as true to-day as at any period in the world's history.

FERRIC ODYLINE INSOLES

WILL PREVENT OR CURE

NEARLY EVERY

FORM OF DISEASE,

INCLUDING CONSUMPTION, LIVER AND KIDNEY TROUBLES, CATARRH, RHEUMATISM, GOUT, NERVOUS COMPLAINTS, PARALYSIS, &c. Stand on ice all day, yet have WARM FEET by wearing

Ferric Odyline Insoles.

PRICE ONLY

50 CTS. PER PAIR.

Cold feet an impossibility, nearly every form of disease permanently cured by FERRIC ODYLINE GARMENTS.

FERRIC ODYLINE.

Mysterious law our world controls,
To man unknown, by all unseen,
But science circumscribed the poles,
And gave us Ferric Odyline.

The ills to which our flesh is heir
Will cease to scourge our human being,
For gaunt disease cannot be where
Is used the Ferric Odyline.

The deadly drugs of other days
Prescribed by honest men have been,
But now the folly of their way,
They see in Ferric Odyline.

Rheumatic pains endured for years,
A Chronic Cough or Hardened Spleen,
And Asthma always disappears
Beneath the Ferric Odyline.

Consumption's glassy eye no more
Shall lighten up the dying scene,
For all her dreaded powers are o'er
When faced with Ferric Odyline.

Neuralgic pains distract the sense,
And sleepless nights may intervene,
But Nature gives her recompense
In soothing Ferric Odyline.

When business cares o'ertax the brain,
And leave the body lank and lean,
Would you your nervous force regain,
Then wear the Ferric Odyline.

However cold the clime may be,
O'er marshes damp or mountains green,
Your feet from Chills are ever free
When soled with Ferric Odyline.

From youth's first dawn to hoary age
The fertile fields of life we glean,
And on the world's historic page
We'll fix the Ferric Odyline.

The price will be returned in every case where they do not give satisfaction.

(Stamps taken.)

Sent postpaid on receipt of 50 cents by the Ferric Odyline M'f'g Co., 842 Broadway, New York. To families, 6 pair for \$2 50. State size wanted and whether for lady or gentleman. Agents wanted in every town.

Use Dr. Scott's Electric Hair and Flesh Brushes, Price \$3 each.

Pall Mall Electric Association, London.
Dr. SCOTT'S ELECTRIC CURLER. 50c.
Sent on Trial, Postpaid.
DR. SCOTT'S ELECTRIC
CRIMPER AND CURLER.
By its aid the hair, beard or moustache can be curled any desired style in from one to two minutes. For ladies it produces the "Langtry Style," the "Patti Bang," the "Montague Curl," and any other form desired by ladies wearing their hair in the fashionable "loose and fluffy" mode. Gentlemen's moustaches and beards curled for the day in a few seconds. A beautiful article: handle of rosewood, other part nickel-plated.
Dr. SCOTT'S ELECTRIC TOOTH BRUSH OF ALL DRUGGISTS.
The finest Tooth Brush ever made, constructed by a new patented process which renders it impossible for Bristles to come out in use. Each of above articles guaranteed and sent on trial, postpaid, on receipt of price, 50 cts., or both for $1. They may be returned if not satisfactory. Canvassing Agents wanted for Dr. SCOTT'S ELECTRIC CORSETS, BRUSHES, BELTS, &c. No risk, quick Sales. GEO. A. SCOTT, 842 Broadway, New York. Sold at Drug and Fancy Stores. Mention paper.

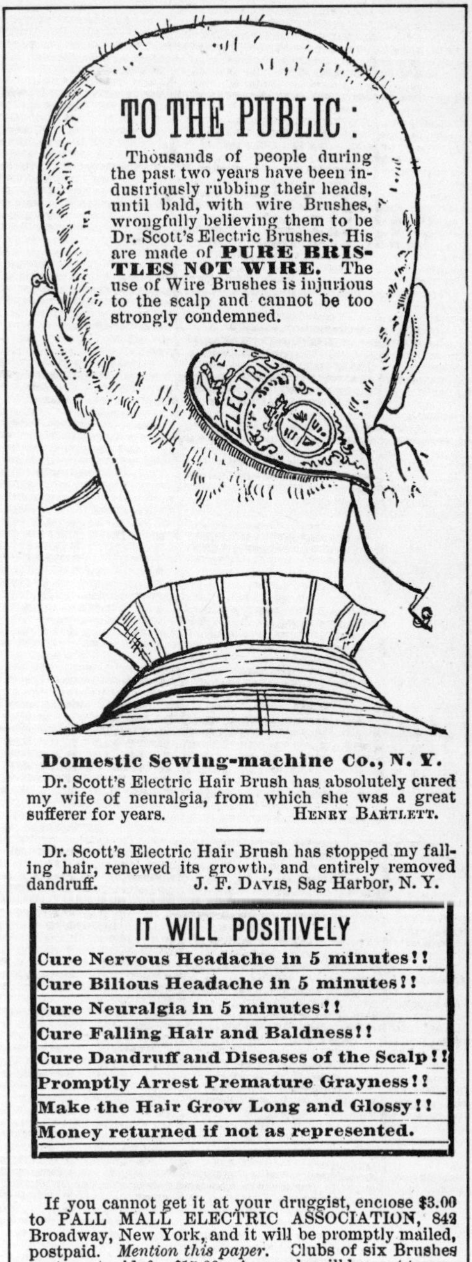

TO THE PUBLIC :
Thousands of people during the past two years have been industriously rubbing their heads, until bald, with wire Brushes, wrongfully believing them to be Dr. Scott's Electric Brushes. His are made of PURE BRISTLES NOT WIRE. The use of Wire Brushes is injurious to the scalp and cannot be too strongly condemned.
ELECTRIC
Domestic Sewing-machine Co., N. Y.
Dr. Scott's Electric Hair Brush has absolutely cured my wife of neuralgia, from which she was a great sufferer for years. HENRY BARTLETT.
Dr. Scott's Electric Hair Brush has stopped my falling hair, renewed its growth, and entirely removed dandruff. J. F. DAVIS, Sag Harbor, N. Y.
IT WILL POSITIVELY
Cure Nervous Headache in 5 minutes!!
Cure Bilious Headache in 5 minutes!!
Cure Neuralgia in 5 minutes!!
Cure Falling Hair and Baldness!!
Cure Dandruff and Diseases of the Scalp!!
Promptly Arrest Premature Grayness!!
Make the Hair Grow Long and Glossy!!
Money returned if not as represented.
If you cannot get it at your druggist, enclose $3.00 to PALL MALL ELECTRIC ASSOCIATION, 842 Broadway, New York, and it will be promptly mailed, postpaid. Mention this paper. Clubs of six Brushes sent, postpaid, for $15.00. A sample will be sent to any Bank or Postmaster for inspection. Agents wanted.

DR. SCOTT'S ELECTRIC GIRDLE FOR MEN.

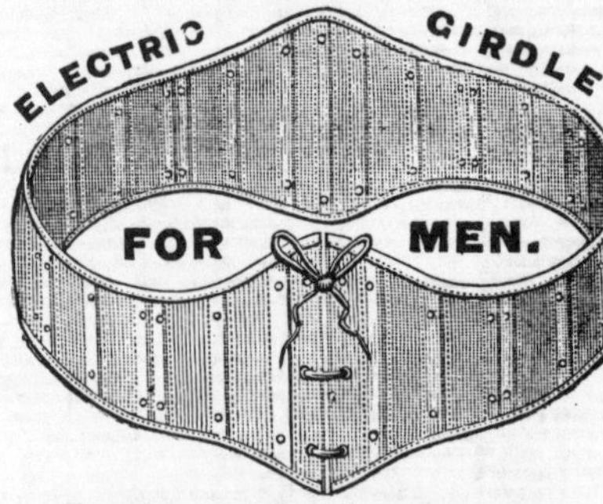

Professional men affirm that there is hardly a disease which Electricity and Magnetism will not benefit or cure.

Dr. W. A. HAMMOND, of N. Y.,

late Surgeon-Gen. of the U. S., an eminent authority, publishes almost miraculous cures made by him with these agencies.

Most of the above Remarks apply equally to

The Electric Girdle for Gentlemen. It is a long felt want, possessing wonderful curative powers and life-giving properties. The debilitated particularly should wear them at once, and those now enjoying robust health should also wear them as a preventative of disease. They brace up and invigorate the whole system, and their vitalizing influence is quickly felt.

As Wonderful as the Telephone and Electric Light.

Beauty! Grace! Symmetry!

Foot and Ankle.

Health! Activity! Vigour!

Every Lady, Gentleman, and Child should wear

The EDSON Electric Garter.

They develope the ANKLE and FOOT into perfect form, support and strengthen the LIMBS, add MARVELLOUS GRACE and elasticity to the step, give GREAT EASE and COMFORT in WALKING, DANCING, SKATING, ROWING or RIDING, maintain and excite healthful circulation, PUT AN END TO ILL-SHAPEN and DWARFED LIMBS and ANKLES, dispel GOUT, RHEUMATIC, and NEURALGIC PAINS, subdue all cramps and stiffness of joints.

Wholly supersedes not only the costly Galvanic and Magnetic Appliances of the day, but every other form of Garter for Ladies' Gentlemen's, or Child's wear. They are worn with all the comfort of the best known Garters. Not more expensive. Beautiful in appearance. Adjusted in a moment. Finished in Finest Silk and Cotton Fabric (usuul Colours) with Stud and Buckle Clasps. Are lasting wear.

Like the Telephone and Electric Light, it has taken time to develope, but is now the success of the day. PRICE:—The Electric Garters in Finest Cotton Webbing, Ladies' or Gent's Size, 75c.; in Silk, $1; Child's Size, (up to eight years) 50c.; in Silk, 75c.

Royal Letters Patent.

Remit by Post-Office Orders or Registered Letter.

Address

LONDON ELECTRIC FABRIC COMPANY,

No. 144 Duane St.,

P. O. Box No. **4048.** **NEW YORK.**

JUDSON'S PERFECT PURITY FILTERS.

Not simply a strainer, but a TRUE FILTER. Fitted with "GALVANO ELECTRIC" FILTERING MEDIUM, which DESTROYS low forms of life and poisons in SOLUTION (wherein lies the greatest danger) as well as in suspension.

Scientists agree that the water supplies of our large cities engender disease. This is the season of the year when Cholera, Typhoid, and kindred diseases are to be most dreaded, and are often directly traceable to the use of impure water. A small outlay for a Filter IN TIME will save life, not to mention the saving in doctor's bills. Judson's Filters received the highest awards at the Inventions Exhibition, London, 1885.

DANIEL JUDSON & SON, Limited, London,

Sole Proprietors and Manufacturers.

AMERICAN HEADQUARTERS, 10 Barclay St., New York.

A. F. FREEMAN, Manager.

Write for complete Filter Pamphlet and Catalogue, sent post free on application.

They who suffer ache and pain,
Need suffer never more again.

A NEW INVENTION.

PLEASANT, CONVENIENT AND EFFICACIOUS.

The Pall Mall Electric Association of London and New-York now introduces to the American public a new invention in Plasters. For three years this remarkable Plaster has been used largely in private practice. Its cures have been so wonderful and so quick that, yielding to the urgent solicitations of prominent physicians, it is now made public.

It combines Electro-Magnetism with all the best qualities of standard porous and other Plasters, and is a really wonderful remedy,

CURING Colds, Coughs and Chest Pains,
Nervous, Muscular and Neuralgic Pains,
Stomach, Kidney and Liver Pains,
Dyspeptic, Malarial and other Pains,
Rheumatism, Gout and Inflammation,
IN ONE TO THREE HOURS.

We unhesitatingly guarantee that it will produce most astonishing results, effecting rapid cures where medicine and all other treatments fail.

TRY ONE TO-DAY, and if not entirely satisfactory, the price will be cheerfully refunded. There is no shock, but a pleasant, genial glow. It cannot injure, but will always do good.

Accept no substitute. If you cannot obtain it promptly at your druggist's, remit price, 25cts., to **Geo. A. Scott, 842 Broadway, New-York,** and it will be mailed, post-paid. 5 sent for $1.00. For ordinary troubles, the 25c. plaster is a quick cure, but in chronic cases of long standing, or where pain is acute, we make special plasters to suit special cases, at $1.00 each. Mention this paper.

It Causes no Sores like Voltaic Plasters.

A REMARKABLE INVENTION!

DR. SCOTT'S

ELECTRIC CIGARETTES

NO MATCHES REQUIRED.

LIGHT ON THE BOX.

The finest Cigarette ever made. **Turkish Tobacco** and **Rice Paper.** They never fail to light without matches in the strongest gale, and for the Theatre, Cab, Carriage, Yachting, Fishing, Hunting, on the Ocean and for home, office, and street use, they will be found **Exceedingly Convenient. No Nicotine** can be taken into the system while smoking these Cigarettes, as in the mouth-piece of each is placed a small wad of absorbent cotton, which strains and eliminates the injurious qualities from the smoke. **Give them one trial.** Price, 10 cents per box of 10. If you cannot get them at your cigar store, hotel, or druggist's, remit us 25 cents, 50 cents, or $1, and we will mail boxes containing 20, 50, or 100 Cigarettes, postpaid. If not entirely satisfactory, we will return the money.

Address:

SCOTT & CHAMBERLIN,

842 BROADWAY, N. Y.

BEWARE OF CHEAP CIGARETTES!

☞ It is a matter of regret that many manufacturers of Tobacco and Cigarettes, devoid of all conscience, are now flooding the market with goods of a most injurious quality. DR. SCOTT'S are guaranteed pure and harmless. $1000 will be paid in every case where it is proven that these Cigarettes are adulterated or contain anything but Pure Tobacco. WE CHALLENGE ANALYSIS. Mention this paper.

RELIABLE AGENTS WANTED IN EVERY TOWN.

RUPTURE

Positively cured in 60 days by **Dr. Horne's Electro-Magnetic Belt-Truss**, combined. Guaranteed the only one in the world generating a continuous *Electric & Magnetic current*. Scientific, Powerful, Durable, Comfortable and Effective in curing Rupture 500 cured in '83. Send Stamp for pamphlet.

ELECTRO-MAGNETIC TRUSS CO., 191 WABASH AVE., CHICAGO

Swindles and Hoaxes

In 1826 the following handbill was circulated in Norwich, England and caused considerable excitement.

St James's Hill, back of the Horse Barracks.

The Public are respectfully informed that Signor CARLO GRAM VILLECROP, the celebrated Swiss Mountain Flyer, from Geneva and Mont Blanc, is just arrived in this City, and will exhibit with a Tyrolese Pole, fifty feet long, his most astonishing Gymnastic Flights, never before witnessed in this country. Signor Villecrop has had the great honour of exhibiting his most extraordinary Feats on the Continent before the King of Prussia, Emperor of Austria, the Grand Duke of Tuscany, and all the resident Nobility in Switzerland. He begs to inform the Ladies and Gentlemen of this City that he has selected St James's Hill and the adjoining hills for his performances, and will first display his remarkable strength in running up the hill with his Tyrolese Pole between his teeth. He will next lay on his back, and balance the same Pole on his nose, chin, and different parts of his body. He will climb upon it with the astonishing swiftness of a cat, and stand on his head at the top; on a sudden he will leap three feet from the Pole without falling, suspending himself by a shenese cord only. He will also walk on his head up and down the hill, balancing the Pole on one foot. Many other feats will be exhibited, in which Signor Villecrop will display to the audience the much-admired art of toppling, peculiar only to the Peasantry of Switzerland. He will conclude his performance by repeated flights in the air, up and down the hill, with a velocity almost imperceptible, assisted only by his Pole, with which he will frequently jump the astonishing distance of Forty and Fifty Yards at a time. Signor Villecrop begs to assure the ladies and gentlemen who honour him with their company that no money will be collected till after the exhibition, feeling convinced that his exertions will be liberally rewarded by their generosity. The Exhibition to commence on Monday, the 28th of August 1826, precisely at half-past five o'clock in the evening.

On the evening of August 28th there were more than twenty thousand people assembled at the foot of the hill. Of course Signor Villecrop did not put in an appearance, for he did not exist except in the minds of the swindlers.

This notice appeared in the English paper "Post Boy" in January, 1699.

IN Clerkenwell Close, where the figure of Mad People are over the gate, Liveth one who by the Blessing of God, cureth all Lunitck distracted or Mad People, he seldom exceeds 3 months in the cure of the maddest Person that comes in his house, several have been cured in a fortnight and some in less time; he has cured several from Bedlam and other mad-houses in and about this City and has conveniency for people of what quality soever. No cure no money. He likewise cureth the dropsy infallibly and has taken away from 10, 12, 15, 20 gallons of water with a gentle preparation. He cureth them that are 100 miles off as well as them that are in town, and if any are desirous they may have a note at his house of several that he hath cured.

Among the worst of the early swindlers were those that used religion to make their profits. This particular ad is from an English newspaper of the mid 1800's.

TO THE LORD'S PEOPLE.—A dear Christian tradesman, who about four months ago drew from the Savings' Bank £60, his all therein, to give to a fellow Christian who urgently required that sum, "thus lending and hoping for nothing again" but from a bountiful "God whose name is Love," is now in WANT OF FORTY POUNDS to pay all demands upon him, ere he accepts a call to the ministry of the Everlasting Gospel, which he believes his Heavenly Father is about to make known unto him. A lady, his friend in Christ the Lord as revealed, in the power of God the Holy Ghost, thus ventures in simple faith to try the door of Providence in his behalf; and would leave the issue in the hands of Him who has heart, hand, breath and purse of men at sovereign command. The smallest help will be gratefully acknowledged by the Advertiser. Address to ——.

From the "Weekly Times" in the 1870's.

WONDERS OF THE HOROSCOPE.—Any person sending an addressed envelope, age, height, colour of hair and eyes, together with 13 stamps, will receive within 24 hours a correct likeness of their future husband or wife, and date of marriage.—Address, A. WEMYSS, 2, Drake-street, Red Lion-square, London.

WONDROUS ARTS.—Your future revealed—Seven years, six stamps; lifetime twelve stamps. State age. Love Charm, sixteen stamps. Medicine for removing Gravel and Private diseases in a few days, without injuring the constitution, sixty stamps. Methralton's Bible Key, twenty-six stamps. Book of Spirits, 408 pages, thirty-two stamps. Millennial Prophecies, Gratis. METHRALTON, the Seer, Daventry.

This ad was the cause of one of the first advertising lawsuits. It ran in the "Pall Mall Gazette" on November 13, 1891.

£100 REWARD

WILL BE PAID BY THE

CARBOLIC SMOKE BALL CO.

To any person who contracts the increasing Epidemic,

INFLUENZA,

Colds, or any diseases caused by taking cold, AFTER HAVING USED the BALL 3 times daily for two weeks according to the printed directions supplied with each Ball.

£1,000

Is deposited with the ALLIANCE BANK, REGENT-STREET, showing our sincerity in the matter. During the last epidemic of Influenza many thousand CARBOLIC SMOKE BALLS were sold as Preventives against this Disease, and in no ascertained case was the disease contracted by those using the CARBOLIC SMOKE BALL.

One CARBOLIC SMOKE BALL will last a family several months, making it the cheapest remedy in the world at the price—10s., post free. The BALL can be RE-FILLED at a cost of 5s. Address :—

CARBOLIC SMOKE BALL CO.,

27, Princes-street, Hanover-sq., London, W.

It seems that a Mrs. Carlill purchased the Smoke Ball, used it as directed for two weeks, and contracted influenza. Upon requesting money from the manufacturers, they declined to pay. In court the Smoke Ball Company offered a variety of pleas, and swore they weren't serious in the ad. In the end Mrs. Carlill collected her hundred pounds.

In 1749, the Duke of Montague, Lord Portman, and some other noblemen were talking about the gullibility of the people, and the Duke offered this wager. Let a man advertise the most impossible thing in the world, and he would find fools enough in London to fill a playhouse and pay handsomely for the privilege of being there. "Surely," said the Earl of Chesterfield, "if a man should say that he would jump into a quart bottle, nobody would believe that." The bet was made and the following advertisement was inserted in the papers of January, 1749.

> AT the New Theatre in the Hay market, on Monday next, the 12th instant, is to be seen a Person who performs the several most surprising things following, viz.—1st. He takes a common walking Cane from any of the Spectators, and thereon plays the music of every Instrument now in use, and likewise sings to surprising perfection.—2dly. He presents you with a common Wine Bottle, which any of the spectators may first examine; this Bottle is placed on a Table in the middle of the Stage, and he (without any equivocation) goes into it, in the sight of all the Spectators, and sings in it: during his stay in the bottle, any Person may handle it, and see plainly that it does not exceed a common Tavern Bottle.—Those on the Stage, or in the Boxes, may come in masked habits (if agreeable to them); and the Performer, if desired, will inform them who they are.—Stage, 7s. 6d. Boxes, 5s. Pit, 3s. Gallery, 2s. Tickets to be had at the Theatre :—To begin at half an hour after six o'clock. The performance continues about two hours and a half.
>
> *Note.*—If any Gentlemen or Ladies (after the above Performance) either single or in company, in or out of mask, is desirous of seeing a representation of any deceased Person, such as Husband or Wife, Sister or Brother, or any intimate Friend of either sex, upon making a gratuity to the Performer, shall be gratified by seeing and conversing with them for some minutes, as if alive; likewise, if desired, he will tell you your most secret thoughts in your past Life, and give you a full view of persons who have injured you, whether dead or alive. For those Gentlemen and Ladies who are desirous of seeing this last part, there is a private Room provided.
>
> These performances have been seen by most of the crowned Heads of Asia, Africa, and Europe, and never appeared public any where but once; but will wait on any at their Houses, and perform as above, for five Pounds each time. A proper guard is appointed to prevent disorder.

On the appointed day the theatre was overflowing with people. When the performer failed to make an appearance, the audience started to riot. The theatre was practically demolished. They gutted the building and carried everything burnable out into the street for a giant bonfire.

As a result of the bottle hoax ad, these advertisements were placed in the local newspapers following the event.

LOST, last Monday night at the Little Play house in the Hay market, a Sword with a gold Hilt and cutting Blade, with a crimson and gold Swordknot tied round the Hilt. Whoever brings it to Mr Chevenix's Toy shop, over against Great Suffolk Street, near Chearing Cross, shall receive thirty Guineas reward, and no Questions asked.

FOUND entangled in the slit of a Lady's demolished smock Petticoat, a gold hilted Sword, of martial length and temper, nothing worse for wear, with the Spey curiously wrought on one side of the blade, and the Scheldt on the other ; supposed to have been stolen from the plump side of a great General, in his precipitate retreat from the Battle of Bottle-Noodles, at Station Foote. Enquire at the Quart Bottle and Musical Cane in Potter's Row.

N.B.—Every word of a certain late advertisement is true, except all the advertisement.

Lately arrived from Ethiopia,

THE most wonderful and surprising Doctor BENIMBE ZAMMANPOANGO, Oculist and Body Surgeon to Emperor of Monoemungi, who will perform on Sunday next, at the little T——— in the Hay market, the following surprising Operations ; viz. 1st, He desires any one of the Spectators only to pull out his own Eyes, which as soon as he has done, the Doctor will shew them to any Lady or Gentleman then present, to convince them there is no Cheat, and then replace them in the Sockets, as perfect and entire as ever. 2dly, He desires any officer or other, to rip up his own Belly, which when he has done, he (without any Equivocation) takes out his Bowels, washes them, and returns them to their place, without the Person's suffering the least hurt. 3dly, He opens the head of a J——— of P———, takes out his Brains, and exchanges them for those of a Calf ; the Brains of a Beau for those of an Ass, and the Heart of a Bully for that of a Sheep : which Operations will render the Persons more sociable and rational Creatures than they ever were in their Lives. And to convince the town that no imposition is intended, he desires no Money until the Performance is over. Boxes, 5 guin. Pit 3. Gallery 2.

N.B.—The famous Oculist will be there, and honest S——— F——— H——— will come if he can. Ladies may come masked, so may Fribbles. The Faculty and Clergy gratis. The Orator would be there, but is engaged.

DON JOHN DE NASAQUITINE, sworn Brother and Companion to the Man that was to have jumped into the Bottle at the Little Theatre in the Hay market, on Monday the 16th past; hereby invites all such as were then disappointed to repair to the Theatre aforesaid on Monday the 30th; and *that* shall be exhibited unto them, which never has heretofore, nor ever will be hereafter seen. All such as shall swear upon the Book of Wisdom that they paid for seeing the Bottle Man will be admitted gratis; the rest at Gotham prices.

To be seen at MR LEADER'S, *the Old Horseshoe, in Wood Street, Cheapside, from Nine till Twelve, and from Four to Seven o' Clock, Lately brought from France,*

A FULL grown MOUSE alive, confined in a small two ounce Phial, the Neck of which is not a quarter of an inch Diameter. This amusing Creature has lived in the Phial three Years and a half without Drink or any Sustenance but Bread only. It cleans out its little Habitation, and hath many other pretty Actions, as surprising as agreeable; but particularly creates wonderful diversion with a Fly, and is allowed to be an extraordinary Curiosity, never before seen in England; at the Expense of 6d. each Person.

Note.—Gentlemen or Ladies who don't chuse to come, it shall be carried to them, by sending a line to MR LEADER.

The Patent Medicines

From American publications of the 1870's and 80's.

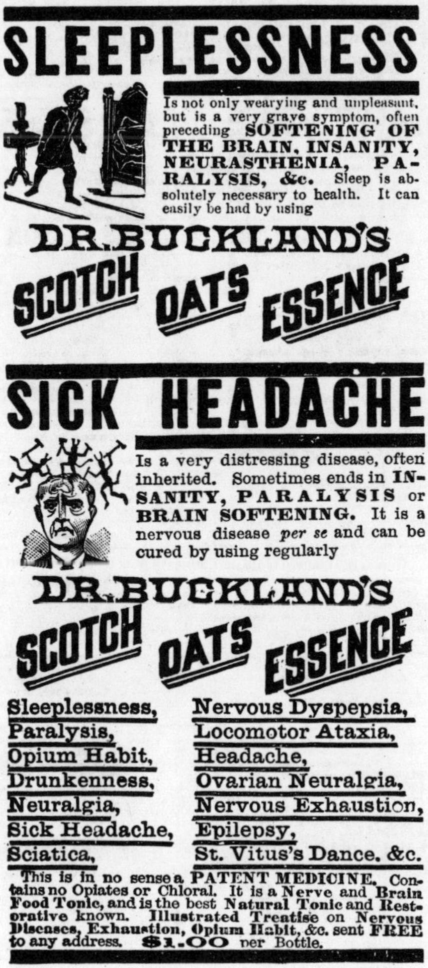

KIDNEY-WORT

The Only Remedy

That Acts at the Same Time on

The Liver, The Bowels and The Kidneys

This combined action gives it wonderful power to cure all diseases.

Why Are We Sick?

Because we allow these great organs to become clogged or torpid, and poisonous humors are therefore forced into the blood that should be expelled naturally.

KIDNEY-WORT WILL CURE

Biliousness, Piles, Constipation, Kidney Complaints and Diseases, Weaknesses and Nervous Disorders.

by causing free action of these organs and restoring their power to throw off disease.

Why Suffer Bilious pains and aches!
Why tormented with Piles, Constipation!
Why frightened over disordered Kidneys!
Why endure nervous or sick headaches!
Why have sleepless nights!

Use **KIDNEY WORT** *and rejoice in health. It is a dry, vegetable compound and* **One package will make six qts of Medicine.** *Get it of your Druggist, he will order it for you. Price,* **$1.00.**

WELLS, RICHARDSON & CO., Proprietors,
(Will send post paid.) Burlington, Vt.

I was so much troubled with catarrh it seriously affected my voice. One bottle of Ely's Cream Balm did the work. My voice is fully restored. — B. F. Liepsner A. M., Pastor of the Olivet Baptist Church, Phila.

ELY BROS., 56 Warren St., N. Y.

COMPOUND OXYGEN The new cure for *Consumption, Asthma, Catarrh, Headache, etc.,* by a *revitalizing process.* **REMARKABLE CURES** *have been made in Chronic and Nervous Diseases, which are attracting wide attention.* **REFER BY PERMISSION** To Rt. Rev. Jno. J. Keane, Bishop of Richmond, Va.; Hon. Wm. D. Kelley, Gen. Fitz Henry Warren, T. S. Arthur, and others who have used and *been largely benefited by this treatment.* **SENT FREE!** Brochure [200 pp.] with many testimonials to *most remarkable cures.* Drs. STARKEY & PALEN, 1112 Girard St., Phila.

WHOOPING-COUGH CURED

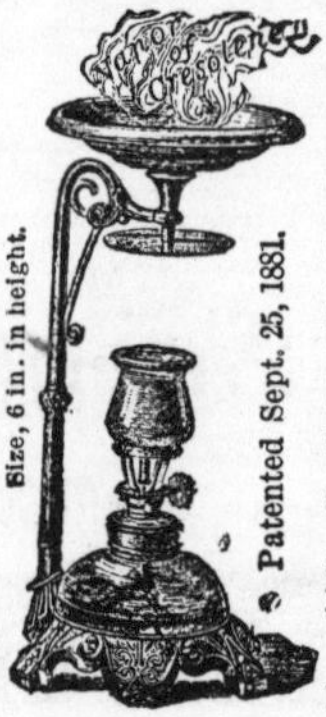

Or Prevented by Page's Vaporizer and Cresolene. We have abundant testimony that Cresolene vaporized in a closed room is an almost infallible remedy for **Whooping-Cough,** for which distressing malady no other assured remedy is known to us. A cure usually effected in five or six days, at a trifling expense and but very little trouble. It is also exceedingly efficient in Asthma, Croup, Catarrh, Diphtheria, Influenza, and Scarlet Fever.

It is a safeguard against the spread of contagion.

Vaporizer complete, including a bottle of Cresolene, $1.50. Ask your druggist for it.

W. H. SCHIEFFELIN & CO.,
SOLE AGENTS,
170-172 William St., New York.

D. LANGELL'S ASTHMA AND CATARRH REMEDY

SOLD BY ALL DRUGGISTS.

Struggled 20 years between life and death with **ASTHMA** or **PHTHISIC,** treated by eminent physicians and receiving no benefit; was compelled during the last 5 years of illness to sit on a chair day and night gasping for breath. Sufferings were beyond description. In despair experimented on myself by compounding roots and herbs and inhaling the medicine thus obtained. I fortunately discovered this **Wonderful Cure for Asthma and Catarrh** warranted to relieve the most stubborn case of **ASTHMA in Five Minutes,** so that the patient can lie down to rest and sleep comfortably. Sufferers from **Asthma, Catarrh, Hay Fever** and all kindred diseases send for free trial pkg.

J. ZIMMERMAN & CO., Wooster, Ohio.
ALBERT IMGARD, Eastern Manager,
866 Sixth Ave., New York City.
FULL SIZE BOX BY MAIL, $1.00.

FITS CURED.

Dr. Brown's great prescription for **Epilepsy** having now been tested in over 10,000 cases without a failure, he has made up his mind to make the ingredients known to all sufferers free of charge.

Address **Dr. O. PHELPS BROWN,**
21 Grand Street, Jersey City, N. J.

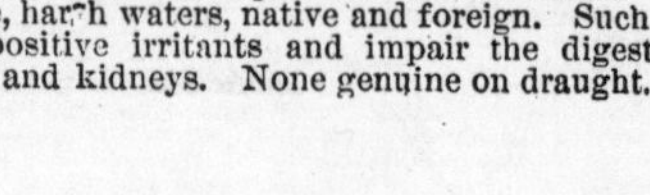

CONGRESS WATER.

Superior to all. Cathartic, alterative. A specific for disorders of the stomach, liver, kidneys, eczema, malaria, and all impurities of the blood. Avoid crude, harsh waters, native and foreign. Such waters are positive irritants and impair the digestive organs and kidneys. None genuine on draught.

As the SHIPS come in they are liable to bring

CHOLERA

which attacks people suddenly and without WARNING.

In such cases no medicine is equal to

PERRY DAVIS' PAIN-KILLER

In INDIA where the CHOLERA is so terrible the natives WORSHIP PERRY DAVIS' PAIN-KILLER and call it the MEDICINE of the GODS, because it is so wonderful in its cures ... It should be in every house---It is invaluable for CHOLERA MORBUS Diarrhoea Dysentery and all BOWEL Complaints.

Perry Davis & Son. Prop^{rs}
Providence, R.I.

THE OPIUM HABIT

Cured without PAIN, EXPOSURE or SLEEPLESSNESS at home, by the method of Dr. H. H. Kane, Author of "Drugs that Enslave," (Pub. Lindsay & Blakiston, Phila.) **Descriptive Book with endorsements by 300 physicians**, description, prices, &c. DR. KANE (formerly Sup't De Quincy Hospital), 164 Fulton Street, New York.

TO CURE MALARIA.

The only medicine with which this disease can be successfully combated is Dr. Kennedy's Favorite Remedy. No person living in a district infected by Malaria, or liable to travel where it is, should neglect the precaution of taking this valuable medicine.

"About three years ago I had an attack of Malaria, which reduced and practically used me up. I dosed awhile without result, until a friend said

'WHY DON'T YOU TRY

Dr. David Kennedy's Favorite Remedy.' I did so and it cleared my blood and rid me of my troubles."

JOSEPH CONGDON, Binghamton, N. Y.

It was in the army that I became for the first time acquainted with the practical meaning of the word malaria. Chills, fever, heat, cold, and mental depression, want of ambition. After leaving the army I suffered from attacks of this general character about half a dozen times a year. I dosed and took quinine until my head swam, but it did not help me. By good luck I gave

Dr. D. Kennedy's Favorite Remedy

a chance to show what it could do for me, and it presently cured me completely. Since using the first bottle I haven't a vestige of the old trouble. C. C. KROMER. Editor Schoharie (N. Y.) Union.

That all forms of malaria can be entirely and radically cured is the experience of hundreds who have treated it with Dr. David Kennedy's Favorite Remedy. Quinine affords temporary relief, but does not cure; and, besides, it induces troubles, quite as serious as those it is intended to abate. All who first enter the tropics, which are especially malarious, will find this medicine a protection while becoming acclimated.

PREPARED BY

Dr. David Kennedy, Rondout, N. Y.

Sold by all Druggists. $1 a Bottle, 6 for $5.

"I owe my Restoration to Health and Beauty to the CUTICURA REMEDIES."

Testimonial of a Boston lady.

DISFIGURING Humors, Humiliating Eruptions, Itching Tortures, Scrofula, Salt Rheum, and Infantile Humors cured by the CUTICURA REMEDIES.

CUTICURA RESOLVENT, the new blood purifier, cleanses the blood and perspiration of impurities and poisonous elements, and thus removes the *cause*.

CUTICURA, the great Skin Cure, instantly allays Itching and Inflammation, clears the Skin and Scalp, heals Ulcers and Sores, and restores the Hair.

CUTICURA SOAP, an exquisite Skin Beautifier and Toilet Requisite, prepared from CUTICURA, is indispensable in treating Skin Diseases, Baby Humors, Skin Blemishes, Chapped and Oily Skin.

CUTICURA REMEDIES are absolutely pure, and the only infallible Blood Purifiers and Skin Beautifiers.

Sold everywhere. Price, Cuticura, 50 cents; Soap, 25 cents; Resolvent, $1.

POTTER DRUG AND CHEMICAL CO., BOSTON, MASS.

"It Saved My Life"

Is a common expression, often heard from those who have realized, by personal use, the curative powers of Ayer's Cherry Pectoral. **I cannot say enough in praise of Ayer's Cherry Pectoral, believing as I do that, but for its use, I should long since have died from lung troubles. — E. Bragdon, Palestine, Tex.

About six months ago I had a severe Hemorrhage of the Lungs, brought on by a distressing Cough, which deprived me of sleep and rest. I had used various cough balsams and expectorants, without obtaining relief. A friend advised me to try

Ayer's Cherry Pectoral.

I did so, and am happy to say that it helped me at once. By continued use this medicine cured my cough, and, I am satisfied, saved my life. — Mrs. E. Coburn, 18 Second st., Lowell, Mass.

I have used Ayer's Cherry Pectoral for over a year, and sincerely believe I should have been in my grave, had it not been for this medicine. It has cured me of a dangerous affection of the lungs, for which I had almost despaired of ever finding a remedy. — D. A. McMullen, Windsor, Province of Ontario.

Ayer's Cherry Pectoral saved my life. Two years ago I took a very severe Cold which settled on my lungs. I consulted physicians, and took the remedies they prescribed, but failed to obtain relief until I began using Ayer's Cherry Pectoral. Two bottles of this medicine completely restored my health. — Lizzie M. Allen, West Lancaster, Ohio.

Ayer's Cherry Pectoral,

Prepared by Dr. J. C. Ayer & Co., Lowell, Mass. Sold by all Druggists. Price $1; six bottles, $5

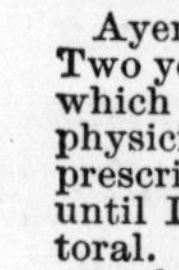

CHEST PAINS

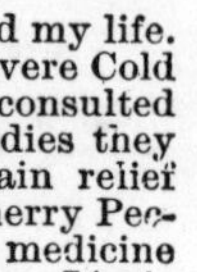

COUGHS, COLDS

Chest Pains, Coughs and Colds, Weak Lungs, Backache, Kidney Pains, Rheumatism, and all Muscular Pains, **relieved in one minute** by the first **Cuticura Anti-Pain Plaster** The and only instantaneous pain-killing strengthening plaster. 25 cents; 5 for $1. At druggists, or of Potter Drug and Chemical Co., Boston.

I Owe My Life.

CHAPTER I.

"I was taken sick a year ago
With bilious fever."

"My doctor pronounced me cured, but I got sick again, with terrible pains in my back and sides, and I got so bad I

Could not move!

I shrunk!

From 228 lbs. to 120! I had been doctoring for my liver, but it did no good, I did not expect to live more than three months. I began to use Hop Bitters.

Directly my appetite returned, my pains left me, my entire system seemed renewed as if by magic, and after using several bottles, I am not only as sound as a sovereign, but weigh more than I did before. To Hop Bitters I owe my life."

Dublin, June 6, '86. R. Fitzpatrick.

CHAPTER II.

"Malden, Mass., Feb. 1, 1886. Gentlemen—
I suffered with attacks of sick headache."

Neuralgia, female trouble, for years in the most terrible and excruciating manner.

No medicine or doctor could give me relief or cure, until I used Hop Bitters.

"The first bottle

Nearly cured me;"

The second made me as well and strong as when a child,

"And I have been so to this day."

My husband was an invalid for twenty years with a serious

"Kidney, liver and urinary complaint.

"Pronounced by Boston's best physicians—

"Incurable!"

Seven bottles of your Bitters cured him and I know of the

"Lives of eight persons"

In my neighborhood that have been saved by your bitters.

And many more are using them with great benefit. "They almost do miracles?"

Mrs. E. D. Slack.

How to Get Sick.—Expose yourself day and night; eat too much without exercise, work too hard without rest, doctor all the time; take all the vile nostrums advertised, and then you will want to know

How to Get Well.—which is answered in three words—Take Hop Bitters.

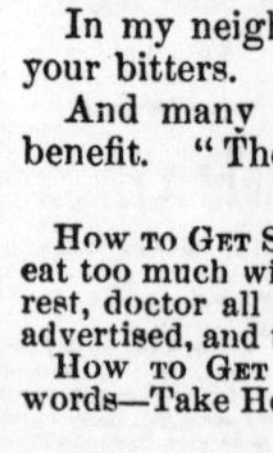

POSITIVELY

NOT INJURIOUS.

For the THROAT and NERVES.

CURE SORE THROAT, NEURALGIA, NERVOUSNESS, HEADACHE, COLDS, AND SLEEPLESSNESS.

Price, 50c. a Box at Druggists or by Mail

ALLEN COCAINE MFG. CO., 1254 Broadway, N. Y.

Geo N Stoddard

Chemist and Druggist.

IS THIS WHAT AILS YOU?

Do you feel generally miserable, or suffer with a thousand and one indescribable bad feelings, both mental and physical?—among them low spirits, nervousness, weariness, lifelessness, weakness, dizziness, feelings of fulness and bloating after eating, or sense of "goneness" or emptiness of stomach in morning, flesh soft and lacking firmness, headache, blurring of eyesight, specks floating before the eyes, nervous irritability, poor memory, chilliness alternating with hot flushes, lassitude, throbbing, gurgling or rumbling sensations in bowels, with heat and nipping pains occasionally, palpitation of heart, short breath on exertion, slow circulation of blood, cold feet, pain and oppression in chest and back, pain around the loins, aching and weariness of the lower limbs, drowsiness after meals but nervous wakefulness at night, languor in the morning and a constant feeling of dread, as if something awful was about to happen?

If you have any or all of the symptoms, send **36** cents to GEO. N. STODDARD, druggist, 1226 Niagara Street, Buffalo, N. Y., and I will tell you what ails you and send you, postpaid, some simple and harmless powders, pleasant to take, and easy directions, which, if you follow, will positively and effectually cure in from one to three weeks' time, no matter how bad you may be. Few have suffered from these causes more than I, and fewer still at my age (48) are in more perfect health than I am now. The same means will cure you.

The Cincinnati CHRISTIAN STANDARD says: "We have seen testimonials from sufferers, and they all verify the good results obtained from his simple remedies. We know Mr. Stoddard personally, and can vouch for the truthfulness of his statements. He has been in business in Buffalo for eighteen years, always doing just as he agreed to. Our readers need have no hesitancy in sending him money."

THE CHRISTIAN AT WORK, New York, says: "We are personally acquainted with Mr. Stoddard, and know that any communication to him will receive prompt and careful attention."

LADIES and the LOSS of the HAIR!

It is much easier to prevent the Hair falling out than it is to renew it, and we guarantee to stop the worst case of falling hair in TEN days by the use of Benton's Hair Grower alone. Ladies have applied to us frequently after having been told that the only way to save their hair was to HAVE the head shaved. If permitted we could refer to many LADIES who to-day are rejoicing in the increased luxuriance of their own NATURAL hair.

Three years ago I had an attack of Typhoid fever, since then my hair has been falling out. I have used one bottle of Benton's Hair Grower, and my hair has ceased coming out, and I believe one bottle of double strength will start a new growth of hair. Mrs. H. M. MOORE, Clinton, Ia.

DEAR SIRS: About one year and a half ago, I bought a bottle of your Hair Grower, and I found that it started out a new growth of hair on my head which has been partially bald for years.

Respectfully yours,
J. H. MALOTT, Mitchell, Ind.

PRICE BY MAIL, $1.00.

Thousands of testimonials, and much interesting matter about the Hair free.

Address THE BENTON HAIR GROWER CO.,

Brainard Block, Cleveland, O.

WHY SUFFER?

When Relief and a Cure can be Assured You by use of **THE ELECTROPOISE**, an **OXYGEN HOME TREATMENT**, which cures disease by an unlimited increase of vitality? NO MEDICINE; no ELECTRICITY. Address for particulars,

Electropoise
(TRADE MARK.)

1425 New York Ave., Washington, D. C.

PARKER'S GINGER TONIC

Ginger, Buchu, Mandrake, Stillingia, and many of the best medicines known are combined in Parker's Ginger Tonic, into a medicine of such varied powers, as to make it the greatest Blood Purifier and the **Best Health & Strength Restorer Ever Used.**

It cures Rheumatism, Sleeplessness, & diseaess of the Stomach, Bowels, Lungs, Liver & Kidneys, & is entirely different from Bitters, Ginger Essences and other Tonics, as it never intoxicates. Hiscox & Co., Chemists, N. Y.

Parker's Hair Balsam.

The Best, Cleanest, and Most Economical Hair Dressing. Never fails to restore the youthful color to gray hair.

50c. and $1 sizes. Large Saving Buying Dollar Size.

OH! HOW BAD I FEEL.

HOW HAPPY AM I!

USE DR. WILBOR'S

COD-LIVER OIL & PHOSPHATES

I didn't, but took those cheap and rancid mixtures recommended as being as good as WILBOR'S, by

MERCENARY DRUGGISTS,

because they make five cents more a bottle on them.

I USED WILBOR'S

PURE COD-LIVER OIL & PHOSPHATES

ALMOST AS PLEASANT AS CREAM.

It cures Consumption, Coughs, Colds, Asthma, Bronchitis, Wasting Diseases and Scrofulous Humors. Be sure, as you value your health, and get the genuine.

Manufactured only by DR. ALEX. WILBOR, Chemist, Boston, Mass. Sold by Druggists.

BUFFALO LITHIA WATER,

FOR BRIGHT'S DISEASE OF THE KIDNEYS,

GOUTY DIATHESIS, NERVOUS DYSPEPSIA, &c.

Dr. Wm. A. Hammond, of New York, Surgeon-General U. S. Army (retired), Professor of Diseases of the Mind and Nervous System in the University of New York, &c.

"I have for some time made use of the Buffalo Lithia Water in cases of affections of the *Nervous System*, complicated with *Bright's Disease of the Kidneys*, or with a *Gouty Diathesis. The results have been eminently satisfactory.* Lithia has for many years been a favorite remedy with me in like cases, but the *Buffalo Water certainly acts better than any extemporaneous solution of the Lithia Salts, and is, moreover, better borne by the stomach.* I also often prescribe it in those cases of *Cerebral Hyperæmia, resulting from overmental work*—in which the condition called *Nervous Dyspepsia* exists—*and generally with marked benefit.*"

Dr. Alfred L. Loomis, of New York, Professor of Institutes and Practice of Medicine, Medical Department University of New York.

"For the past four years I have used the Buffalo Lithia Water in the treatment of Chronic *Interstitial Nephritis** occurring in *Gouty* and *Rheumatic* subjects, with the most *marked benefit.* In all Gouty and Rheumatic Affections I regard it as highly efficacious."

[* The third stage of Bright's Disease of the Kidneys.]

Water in cases of one dozen half-gallon bottles, $5 per case, at the springs. Springs pamphlet sent to any address. WATER FOR SALE BY LEADING DRUGGISTS.

THOMAS F. GOODE, Proprietor,

BUFFALO LITHIA SPRINGS, VIRGINIA.

Imperial Granum
THE GREAT MEDICINAL FOOD
THIS
WORLD
RENOWNED
DIETETIC PREPARATION
IS PRESENTED WITH THE ASSURANCE THAT IT IS THE SAFEST, MOST NICELY PREPARED AND RELIABLE MEDICINAL FOOD THAT SCIENTIFIC RESEARCH CAN YIELD. IT HAS ACQUIRED THE REPUTATION OF BEING AN ALIMENT THE STOMACH SELDOM, IF EVER, REJECTS, CONDITION NOT EXCEPTED: AND, WHILE IT WOULD BE DIFFICULT TO CONCEIVE OF ANYTHING IN FOOD MORE DELICIOUS, OR MORE SOOTHING AND NOURISHING AS AN ALIMENT FOR INVALIDS, AND THE AGED; AND FOR THE GROWTH AND PROTECTION OF CHILDREN. ITS RARE MEDICINAL EXCELLENCE IN INANITION DUE TO MAL-ASSIMILATION, CHRONIC, GASTRIC, AND INTESTINAL DISEASES, (ESPECIALLY IN CHOLERA, DYSENTERY, CHRONIC DIARRHŒA, AND CHOLERA INFANTUM,) HAS BEEN INCONTESTABLY PROVEN: — OFTEN IN INSTANCES OF CONSULTATION OVER PATIENTS WHOSE DIGESTIVE ORGANS WERE REDUCED TO SUCH A LOW AND SENSITIVE CONDITION THAT THE GRANUM WAS THE ONLY THING THE STOMACH WOULD TOLERATE, WHEN LIFE SEEMED DEPENDING ON ITS RETENTION.
"NONPAREIL"
UT PROSIM
SUPERIOR NUTRITION
THE LIFE
TRADE MARK REGISTERED JUNE 5TH 1877
SOLD BY DRUGGISTS
SHIPPING DEPOT, JOHN CARLE & SONS. New York.

Personal Ads

Personal and matrimonial advertisements were most prevalent in the early days of newspaper advertising. They were certainly more colorful and more interesting reading than the majority of early product and service ads.

Although the actual advertisements on the following pages appear to be extreme, they are actually quite typical of the period.

This ad for a runaway servant, who evidently took half the household with her, ran in the English publication "Mercurius Politicus" of May, 1658.

A Black-haired Maid, of a middle stature, thick set, with big breasts, having her face full marked with the small-pox, calling herself by the name of *Nan* or *Agnes Hobson*, did, upon Monday, the 28 of May, about six o'Clock in the morning, steal away from her Ladies house in the Pal-Mall, a mingle-coloured wrought Tabby gown of Deer colour and white; a black striped Sattin Gown with four broad bone-black silk Laces, and a plain black watered French Tabby Gown; Also one Scarlet-coloured and one other Pink-coloured Sarcenet Peticoat, and a white watered Tabby Wastcoat, plain; Several Sarcenet, Mode, and thin black Hoods and Scarfs, several fine Holland Shirts, a laced pair of Cuffs and Dressing, one pair of Pink-coloured Worsted Stockings, a Silver Spoon, a Leather bag, &c. She went away in greyish Cloth Wastcoat turned, and a Pink-coloured Paragon upper Peticoat, with a green Tammy under one. If any shall give notice of this person or things at one *Hopkins*, a Shoomaker's, next door to the Vine Tavern, near the Pal-mall end, near Charing Cross, or at Mr *Ostler's*, at the Bull Head in Cornhill, near the Old Exchange, they shall be rewarded for their pains.

From the same publication a year later.

A Small black NAG, some ten or eleven years old, no white at all, bob-Tailed, wel forehanded, somewhat thin behind, thick Heels, and goeth crickling and lamish behind at his first going out; the hair is beat off upon his far Hip as broad as a twelvepence; he hath a black leather Saddle trimmed with blew, and covered with a black Calves-skin, its a little torn upon the Pummel; two new Girths of white and green thread, and black Bridle, the Rein whereof is sowed on the off side, and a knot to draw it on the near side, Stoln out of a field at *Chelmsford*, 21 *February* instant, from Mr *Henry Bullen*. Whosoever can bring tidings to the said Mr *Bullen*, at *Bromfield*, or to Mr *Newman* at the Grocer's Arms in *Cornhil*, shall have 20s. for his pains.

This ad appeared in the "London Gazette" on December 22, 1679. Though the villains were never discovered, the beating was probably a reprisal for Dryden's writings, "Essay on Satire," which offended several people.

WHEREAS *John Dryden*, Esq., was on Monday, the 18th instant, at night, barbarously assaulted and wounded, in Rose Street in Covent Garden, by divers men unknown; if any person shall make discovery of the said offenders to the said Mr Dryden, or to any Justice of the Peace, he shall not only receive Fifty Pounds, which is deposited in the hands of Mr Blanchard, Goldsmith, next door to Temple Bar, for the said purpose, but if he be a principal or an accessory in the said fact, his Majesty is graciously pleased to promise him his pardon for the same.

The following two ads are from the "London Gazette" in 1688.

WHEREAS Mr Herbert Jones, Attorney-at-Law in the Town of Monmouth, well known by being several years together Under-Sheriff of the same County, hath of late divers times robbed the Mail coming from that town to London, and taken out divers letters and writs, and is now fled from justice, and supposed to have sheltered himself in some of the new-raised troops. These are to give notice that whosoever shall secure the said Herbert Jones, so as to be committed in order to answer these said crimes, may give notice thereof to Sir Thomas Fowles, goldsmith, Temple-bar, London, or to Mr Michael Bohune, mercer, in Monmouth, and shall have a guinea's reward.

WHEREAS a Gentleman was, on the eighteenth at night, mortally wounded near Lincoln's Inn, in Chancery Lane, in view as is supposed of the coachman that set him down: these are to give notice that the said coachman shall come in and declare his knowledge of the matter; if any other person shall discover the said coachman to John Hawles, at his chamber in Lincoln's Inn, he shall have 5 guineas reward.

Highwaymen seemed to do a thriving business during this period. This ad ran in the "Flying Post" of October 27, 1696.

WHEREAS six gentlemen (all of the same honourable profession), having been more than ordinary put to it for a little pocket-money, did, on the 14th instant, in the evening near Kentish town, borrow of two persons (in a coach) a certain sum of money, without staying to give bond for the repayment: And whereas fancy was taken to the hat, peruke, cravate, sword and cane, of one of the creditors, which were all lent as freely as the money: these are, therefore, to desire the said six worthies, how fond soever they may be of the other loans, to unfancy the cane again, and send it to Will's Coffee-house, in Scotland yard; it being too short for any such proper gentlemen as they are, to walk with, and too small for any of their important uses and withal, only valuable as having been the gift of a friend.

This want ad in the "Collection for the Improvement of Husbandry and Trade" in the late 1600's.

—— I want an Englishman that can tolerably well speak French (if Dutch too so much the better), and that will be content to sit at home keeping accounts almost his whole time, and give good security for his fidelity, and he shall have a pretty good salary.

From the English newspaper "Tatler" of August 10, 1710.

WHEREAS an ignorant Upstart in Astrology has publicly endeavoured to persuade the world that he is the late John Partridge, who died the 28 of March 1718, these are to certify all whom it may concern, that the true John Partridge was not only dead at that time but continues so to the present day. Beware of counterfeits, for such are abroad.

Public combat between women seems to have been a routine occurrence in the early 1700's. The following challenge and reply were published in an English newspaper in 1722.

CHALLENGE.—I, Elizabeth Wilkinson, of Clerkenwell, having had some words with Hannah Hyfield, and requiring satisfaction, do invite her to meet me upon the stage, and box me for three guineas; each woman holding half a crown in each hand, and the first woman that drops the money to lose the battle.

ANSWER.—I, Hannah Hyfield, of Newgate Market, hearing of the resoluteness of Elizabeth Wilkinson, will not fail, *God willing*, to give her more blows than words, desiring home blows, and from her no favour; she may expect a good thumping!

In the "Daily Post" of July 17, 1728 we find similar advertisements for a forthcoming brawl between a European championess and an ass-woman.

AT *Mr. Stokes' Amphitheatre* in Islington Road, this present Monday, being the 7 of October, will be a complete Boxing Match by the two following Championesses :—Whereas I, Ann Field, of Stoke Newington, ass-driver, well known for my abilities in boxing in my own defence wherever it happened in my way, having been affronted by Mrs. Stokes, styled the European Championess, do fairly invite her to a trial of the best skill in boxing for 10 pounds, fair rise and fall; and question not but to give her such proofs of my judgment that shall oblige her to acknowledge me Championess of the Stage, to the entire satisfaction of all my friends.

I, Elizabeth Stokes, of the City of London, have not fought in this way since I fought the famous boxing woman of Billingsgate 29 minutes and gained a complete victory (which is six years ago); but as the famous Stoke Newington ass-woman dares me to fight her for the 10 pounds, I do assure her I will not fail meeting her for the said sum, and doubt not that the blows which I shall present her with will be more difficult for her to digest, than any she ever gave her asses. *Note.* —A man known by the name of Rugged and Tuff, challenges the best man of Stoke Newington to fight him for one guinea to what sum they please to venture. *N.B.*—Attendance will be given at one, and the encounter to begin at four precisely. There will be the diversion of cudgel-playing as usual.

The following is one of the earliest known instances of advertising being used in relation to a private quarrel. From the "Daily Post" of January, 1720.

WHEREAS an advertisement was lately put in Heathcote's Halfpenny Post, by way of challenge for me to meet a person (whose name to me is unknown) at Old Man's Coffeehouse near Charing Cross, the 28 instant in order to hear that said person make out his assertions in that Dialogue we had in Palace Yard, the 11th of November 1718, This will let that person know that as he would not then tell me his name, nor put it to his advertisement, I conclude he is ashamed to have it in print. When he sends me his name in writing, that I may know who to ask for, I shall be willing to meet him at any convenient time and place, either by ourselves or with two friends on each side; till then I shall have neither list nor leisure to obey his nameless summons. ROBERT CURTIS.

Southwark, Jan. 13th, 1719–20.

This public apology ran in an English newspaper in the early 1700's.

Bristol, January 19, 173$\frac{2}{3}$.

WHEREAS on or about the 10th day of November last I did say in the Presence of Several People, That Anthony Coller, living at the Sign of the Ship and Dove in the Pithay in Bristol, was sent to Newgate for putting Live Toads in his Beer, in order to fine it; I do solemnly declare, That I never knew any such Thing to have been done by the said Coller nor do I believe he was ever guilty of the aforesaid or any like Practice; I am therefore heartily sorry for what I have said and hereby ask Pardon for the same of the above said Person, who, I fear, has been greatly injur'd by the unguarded Tongue of JOSEPH ROBINS.

Ads like the following were very prevalent in the mid 1700's. From the English newspapers "General Advertiser" and "Daily Advertiser."

WHEREAS a lady last Saturday evening at the playhouse in Drury Lane in one of the left-hand boxes, was observed to take particular notice of a gentleman who sat about the middle of the pit, and as her company would be esteemed the greatest favour, she is humbly desired to send him directions, where and in what manner she would be waited upon, and direct the said letter to be left for P. M. Z. at the Portugal Coffee house near the Exchange.

WHEREAS a young lady was at Covent Garden playhouse last Tuesday night, and received a blow with a square piece of wood on her breast; if the lady be single and meet me on Sunday at two o'clock, on the Mall in St James's Park, or send a line directed for A. B., to Mr Jones's, at the Sun Tavern at St Paul's Churchyard, where and when I shall wait on her, to inform her of something very much to her advantage on honourable terms, her compliance will be a lasting pleasure to her most obedient servant.

IF the young gentleman who came into the Oratorio last Wednesday and by irresistible address gained a place for the lady he attended is yet at liberty, Sylvia may still be happy. But, alas! her mind is racked when she reflects on all the tender anxiety he discovered (or she fears she saw) in all his care of her that evening. How much, how deep was all his attention engaged by that too lovely, too happy fair! At all events an interview is earnestly sought, even if it be to talk to me of eternally lasting sorrow. Notice how to direct to him shall not want gratitude. He may remember a circumstance of a lady's mentioning as he passed the sentimental look and sweetness of his eye.

The individual who ran this ad in the "Daily Post" of January, 1739 seems to have been unjustly punished. He certainly possessed a considerable amount of faith if he believed that the villains would expose themselves and give him the "satisfaction of a gentleman."

WHEREAS on Saturday the 12th instant between six and seven at night, a gentleman coming along the north side of Lincolns Inn fields was set upon by three persons unknown and receiv'd several blows before he could defend himself, upon a presumption, as they said that he was the author of a Satire call'd "the Satirist." This is to inform them that they are greatly mistaken, and that the insulted person is neither the author of that Satire nor of any Satire or Poem whatever, nor knows what the said Satire contains: and therefore has reason to expect, if they are Gentlemen, that they will not refuse him a meeting, by a line to A. Z., to be left at the Bar of Dick's Coffee House, Temple Bar, in order to make him such atonement as shall be judged reasonable by the friends on each side; otherwise he is ready to give any one of them, singly, the satisfaction of a Gentleman, when and wherever shall be appointed, so as he may not have to deal with Numbers.

This rather unique idea is from the "Edinburgh Courant" of October 28, 1758.

GLASGOW, *Octob.* 23, 1758.

WE Robert M'Nair and Jean Holmes having taken into consideration the way and manner our daughter Jean acted in her Marriage, that she took none of our advice, nor advised us before she married, for which reason we discharged her from our Family, for more than Twelve Months; and being afraid that some or other of our Family may also presume to marry without duly advising us thereof, We, taking the affair into our serious consideration, hereby discharge all and every one of our Children from offering to marry without our special advice and consent first had and obtained; and if any of our Children should propose or presume to offer Marriage to any, without as aforesaid our advice and consent, they in that case shall be banished from our Family Twelve Months, and if they should go so far as to marry without our advice and consent, in that case they are to be banished from the Family Seven Years; but whoever advises us of their intention to marry and obtains our consent, shall not only remain Children of the Family, but also shall have a due proportion of our Goods, Gear, and Estate, as we shall think convenient, and as the bargain requires; and further if any one of our Children shall marry clandestinely, they, by so doing, shall lose all claim or title to our Effects, Goods, Gear or Estate; and we intimate this to all concerned, that none may pretend ignorance.

The following ad from a "Gentleman of Honour" ran in the "Morning Post" in 1775.

A GENTLEMAN of Honour and Property, having in his disposal at present a young Lady of good Family, with a fortune of Sixty Thousand Pounds, on her Marriage with his approbation, would be very happy to treat with a Man of Fashion and Family, who may think it worth his while to give the Advertiser a Gratuity of Five thousand pounds on the day of Marriage. As this is no common advertisement, it is expected no Gentleman will apply whose Family and Connections will not bear the strictest enquiry. The Advertiser having always lived retired from the World, immersed in business, is unacquainted with those of that Rank of Life that the Lady's fortune entitles her to be connected with, for which reason he has made this public application. Letters addressed to L. M., at Tom's Coffee House, Devereux Court, near the Temple, mentioning real Name, and places of Abode, will punctually be attended to.

It is hard to imagine that this appeal for a benefactor proved successful for A. Z. From the "St. James's Chronicle" of July, 1772, this ad is typical of numerous requests for money without collateral that were published during this period.

WANTED immediately, Fifteen Hundred or Two Thousand Pounds by a person not worth a Groat, who having neither Houses, Lands, Annuities or public Funds, can offer no other Security than that of simple Bond, bearing simple interest and engaging the Repayment of the Sum borrowed in five, six or seven Years, as may be agreed upon by the Parties. Whoever this may suit (for it is hoped it will suit somebody) by directing a line to A. Z. in Rochester, shall be immediately replied to or waited on, as may appear necessary.

In the English paper "Morning Post" of 1774, a gigolo openly advertises his services.

A YOUNG Gentleman of the most liberal education and a genteel Address, would be happy in having an opportunity of devoting his services to a Lady of real fashion and fortune, who may wish to have some particular deficiencies thoroughly supplied, without subjecting herself to any disagreeable restraint. Any lady to whom such an offer may be suitable, will receive the fullest Explanation, in answer to a letter addressed to A. X. Turk's head Coffee House, Strand.

Also from the "Morning Post" of the same year we find this offer of sex for money.

A LADY wishes to borrow One Hundred Pounds. The Security, though personal, may probably be very agreeable to a single Gentleman of spirit. Every particular will be communicated with Candour and Sincerity, where confidence is so far reposed as to give the real Name and Address of the party willing to oblige the Advertiser. Gentlemen of real Fortune and liberal Sentiments, and those only, are requested to address a line to Y. N. at Mr Dyke's, Cross Street, Long-Acre.

This quaint request for a pregnant woman ran in the "Public Advertiser" in 1776.

A GENTLEMAN who hath filled two succeeding seats in Parliament, is near sixty years of age, lives in great splendour and hospitality, and from whom a considerable Estate must pass if he dies without issue, hath no objection to marry any Widow or single Lady, provided the party be of genteel birth, polite manners, and five, six, seven, or eight Months gone in her Pregnancy.

Letters directed to —— Brecknock, Esq., at Will's Coffee House, facing the Admiralty, will be honoured with due attention, secrecy, and every possible mark of respect.

Money, the sincerest of all friends, was probably the object of this particular ad which ran in an English paper in 1778.

WANTED immediately, the most difficult thing to be met with in the world, A SINCERE FRIEND, by a person, who, though in the meridian of life, has outlived all he had. He wishes to meet with a Person in whom he may repose the most implicit Confidence; a Person who has a good heart, and abilities to second that goodness of heart; who will give his advice cordially, and assistance readily. The advertiser is a person in a genteel situation of life; has a decent income, but is at present so circumstanced as to want a sincere friend.—Any Person willing (from principles of Friendship, not Curiosity) to reply to the above, by directing a line to T. S., at Mr Sharp's, stationer, facing Somerset House, Strand, will be immediately waited on or properly replied to.

From an Irish newspaper of the early 1800's.

RUN AWAY FROM PATRICK M'DALLAGH.—Whereas my wife Mrs Bridget M'Dallagh, is again walked away with herself, and left me with her four small children, and her poor old blind mother, and nobody else to look after house and home, and, I hear, has taken up with Tim Guigan, the lame fiddler—the same that was put in the stocks last Easter for stealing Barday Doody's gamecock.—This is to give notice, that I will not pay for bite or sup on her or his account to man or mortal, and that she had better never show the mark of her ten toes near my home again.

PATRICK M'DALLAGH.

N.B. Tim had better keep out of my sight.

From an English paper of the same period.

TO INDEPENDENT GENTLEMEN.—Wanted by a respectable, modest young man, who can produce a cubic yard of testimonials, a living without a master—that is, he wishes to become a companion to some gentleman, and be his factotum. He can ride, shoot, sing, fish (but never better than his patron without he is wanted), keep accounts, see that servants do their duty, do twenty other things, equally necessary in this life, and make it his whole duty to please and be pleased. Any one seriously wishing such a person, may address, post paid to Z., to be left at ——.

Mr. R was evidently not very particular about his dinner guests, for this ad ran in the "Daily Advertiser" in 1798.

MR. R—— of Stanhope Street, presents his most respectful Compliments to the Gentlemen who did him the honour of eating a couple of roasted Chickens, drinking sundry tankards of ale, and three bottles of old Madeira at his house, on Monday night.

In their haste they took away the Tankard, to which they are heartily welcome; to the Tablespoons and the light Guineas which were in an old red morocco pocket-book, they are also heartily welcome; but in the said Pocket-book there were several loose Papers, which consisted of private Memorandums, Receipts, etc. can be of no use to his kind and friendly Visitors, but are important to him: he therefore hopes and trusts they will be so polite as to take some opportunity of returning them.

For an old family Watch, which was in the same Drawer, he cannot ask on the same terms; but if any could be pointed out by which he could replace it with twice as many heavy Guineas as they can get for it, he would gladly be the Purchaser. W. R.

A few nights later, a packet and a letter were left at his doorstep. The papers and book were returned, and the letter went on to thank him for his hospitality, and inform him that the watch had already been melted down. The writer also mentioned that he and his friends would be glad to visit him again anytime.

From a Maryland newspaper in 1771.

Bush Creek, Frederick's County, Maryland, Oct. 11, 1771.

RUN away from the subscriber, a Servant Maid named Sarah Wilson, but has changed her name to Lady Susanna Carolina Matilda, which made the public believe that she was her Majesty's Sister; she has a blemish in her right Eye, black rolled Hair, stoops in her shoulders, makes a common practice of writing and marking her cloaths with a Crown and a B. Whoever secures the said Servant Woman, or takes her home, shall receive five Pistoles, besides all cost and charges. WILLIAM DEVALL.

I entitle Michael Dalton to search the city of Philadelphia and from thence to Charles-Town, for the said Woman. W. D.

Another "runaway" advertisement ran in a Raleigh, N. C. paper in February, 1815.

TWENTY-FIVE DOLLARS REWARD.

RAN away from Raleigh, a month or two ago, a mulatto man, named *Anthony*, well known in Raleigh, and many parts of the State, as having been, for several years, the body servant of General Jones, and mine lately as a pressman and news-carrier in the Star office. Anthony is about twenty-five or twenty-six years of age, five feet eight or ten inches high, is a mongrel white, has a tolerably large aquiline nose, bushy hair, a scar on one of his cheeks; when in good humour has a pleasing countenance.

He works and walks fast, is lively and talkative, full of anecdote, which he tells in character with much humour; is an excellent pressman, indifferent at distributing types, a tolerable carpenter and joiner, a plain painter, an excellent manager of horses, drives well and rides elegantly, having been accustomed to race riding; is fond of cockfighting (and of man-fighting when drunk), and is said to *heel* and *pit* with skill; he can bleed and pull teeth, knows something of medicines, is a rough barber, a bad but conceited cook, a good sawyer, can lay bricks, has worked in the corn fields, and can scratch a little on the fiddle.

He can do many other things; and what he cannot do, he *pretends* to have a knowledge of. His trades and qualities are thus detailed, because his vanity will undoubtedly lead to a display of them. His master-vice, or rather, the parent of all his vices, is a fondness for *strong drink*, though sometimes he will abstain for months. His clothes cannot be described, but he carried away few or none, and 'tis expected will appear shabbily. He is an artful fellow, and if taken up will tell a most plausible story, and possibly show a forged pass.

The American paper "Connecticut Courant" in 1806 carries this warning from a thankful woman.

EAST WINDSOR, U.S.

THOMAS Hutchins has advertised, that I have absented myself from *his bed and board*, and forbid all persons trusting me on his account, and cautioned all persons against making me any payment on his account. I now advertise the public, that the same Thomas Hutchins came as a fortune-teller into this town about a year ago, with a recommendation, which, with some artful falsehoods, induced me to marry him. Of the four wives he had before me, the last he quarrelled away; how the other three came by their deaths, he can best inform the public: but I caution all widows or maidens against marrying him, be their desire for matrimony ever so strong. Should he make his advances under a feigned name, they may look out for a little, strutting, talkative, feeble, meagre, hatchet-faced fellow, with spindle shanks, and a little warped in the back. THANKFUL HUTCHINS.

From the same period we find this offer made by a mad and obviously rather dumb woman.

$100 REWARD—For the apprehension of Lewis Turtle, a tall man, about 50 years, has considerable money and a high forehead, long face and lantern jawed man, a bad man, with a fist like a giant, and has often beat me, and I want him to end his days in the Penitentiary where he belongs, and he wears a grey coat, with a very large mouth, and one blue eye, and one blind blue eye, and a hideous looking man, and now living with the 7th woman, and me having one child to him, and he has gone off, and I want him brought slap up in the law, with blue pants. He ought to be arrested and has a $100 of my money, and a bald headed rascal, full of flattery and receipt, and she is a bad woman, and her little girl calls him "papa" and is called Eliza Jane Tillis, and a boy blind of one eye, and he is not a man who has got any too much sense, nor her. And he stole $100 from me, and some of my gold and silver, and ought to be caught and I will never live with him again, no never, he is a disgrace. And I would like to have him caught up and compelled to maintain me and his child, as I am his lawful wedded wife, and have the certificate of marriage in my possession.

NANCY TURTLE.

A good servant was evidently hard to find judging from this ad from a Syracuse paper in 1869.

WANTED—A Good SERVANT GIRL to whom the highest wages will be paid. Having had great difficulty in procuring good help, on account of the misfortune of having seven small children, we will poison, drown, or otherwise make away with four of them on application of a first class servant girl. Apply at the office of this paper.

This ad for a mistress ran in a Paris newspaper in the 1850's.

A gentleman in his twenty-sixth year, tired of the dissipation of the great world, is forming a comfortable establishment in one of the least frequented quarters of the city. His domestics are a coachman, cook, three footmen and a chambermaid. He is in search of a young girl of good family to improve this honourable situation : she must be well educated, accomplished, and of an agreeable figure, and will be entertained in the quality of *demoiselle de compagnie*. She shall receive the utmost attention from the household, and be as well served in every respect as, or even better than, if she were its mistress.

The following question and answer ran in the "Telegraph" in the 1870's.

THE lady who travelled from Bedford to London by Midland train on the night of the 4th inst., can now MEET the GENTLEMAN who shared with her the contents of his railway luncheon basket. She enjoys the recollection of that pleasant meal, and would like to know if he is going on another journey. Will keep any appointment made at the Criterion in Piccadilly.—Answer to A.

A. will meet you at the Criterion, on Wednesday, at three. Am going on another journey shortly, and will provide luncheon-basket.—F. M.

From the "Telegraph" in 1874.

MARY ANN C.—Do return home. You labour under an illusion. What you wish to accuse me with does not exist. This I solemnly declare. I have at last a good position, but am so wretched that I cannot attend to my duties properly. Many happier returns of the 1st. God's blessing be with thee, and that He may tend thy heart to believe me in truth. Put six years of love and happiness against your accusation, and you must feel that you are wrong. Oh, you are very, very wrong. Do write and give me an appointment, so that happiness may be re-established. You must be very unhappy, but for God's sake do not be so strong-minded. My love and devotion are unaltered. For your own peace, my sweet, pretty, good wife, come back. When death parts it is sad enough, but to part while living, and without true cause, creates and leaves wretchedness to both. Come back to your unhappy but true-loving husband.

Levi Rockwell used poetry to explain his problems in this ad from a Connecticut paper in 1853.

Julia, my wife, has grown quite rude ;
She has left me in a lonesome mood;
She has left my board,
She has took my bed,
She has gave away my meat and bread,
She has left me in spite of friends and church,
She has carried with her all my shirts.
Now ye who read this paper,
Since she cut this reckless caper,
I will not pay one single fraction
For any debt of her contraction.

LEVI ROCKWELL.

East Windsor, Conn. Aug. 4, 1853.

More of the same from American papers of the 1870's.

WHEREAS I, Daniel Clay, through misrepresentation, was induced to post my wife, Rhoda, in the papers ; now I beg leave to inform the public, that I have again taken her to wife, after settling all our domestic broils in an amicable manner ; so that everything, as usual, goes on like clockwork.

Divorc'd like scissars rent in twain,
Each mourn'd the rivet out :
Now whet and riveted again,
They'll make the old shears cut.

NOTICE.

WHEREAS my husband Chas. F. Sandford, has thought proper to post me, and accuse me of having left his bed and board without cause, etc., I wish to make it known that the said Charlie never had a bed, the bed and furniture belonging to me, given to me by my father ; the room and board he pretended to furnish me were in Providence, where he left me alone, while he staid at the Valley with his "Ma." He offered me $200 to leave him and go home, telling at the same time that I could not stay at the place he had provided for me, and as I have never seen the named sum, I suppose he will let me have it if I can earn the amount. It was useless for Charlie to warn the public against trusting me on his account, as my father has paid my bills since my marriage, as before.

Moral.—Girls, never marry a man not weaned from his "Ma," and don't marry the whole family.

ELEANOR J. SANDFORD.

North Providence, July 1, 1871.

From the "Morning Post" in 1775.

To the Ladies on Money Affairs.

WHEREAS there are sundry Ladies who have Two, Three, or Four thousand pounds, or even more Money at their command, and who, from not knowing how to dispose of the same to the greatest advantage, but by living on the Small Interests which the stocks produce, afford them but a scanty Maintenance, especially to those who have been accustomed to Affluence, and would wish to live so still; the Advertiser (who is a Gentleman of independent Fortune, strict Honour and Character, and above any other reward than the pleasure of serving the Sex) acquaints such Ladies, that if they will favour him with their Name and Address, so as he may wait on them as opportunity best suits, he will put them into a Method by which they may, without any Trouble, and with an absolute Certainty, place out their Money, so as for it to produce them a clear and lawful interest of Ten or Twelve per cent, and that too on equally as good and safe Securities as if in the Funds, or on Mortgage at the common low interest, etc.

Please to direct to R. J. Esq. at the Turks Head Coffee house, opposite Catharine Street, in the Strand, and the same will be duly attended to.

FEMALE COMPANION.

A LADY of independent Fortune and liberal Sentiments would be glad if, in procuring to herself an agreeable Companion she could at the same time relieve from Distress, and perhaps prevent from utter Ruin, some still deserving although unfortunate fair one; for she can make allowance for the frailty of her own Sex, and knows the base arts of the other; in a word, a *single faux pas* will be no objection, provided there remain a virtuous Disposition, and that the person wanted be good-natured, affable, and sincere in the account she may give of herself, which for that purpose may at first be anonymous. She must also possess the usual accomplishments required by a good Education; know something of Music, have an agreeable Voice, and a genteel Person, not under twenty nor above the age of twenty-five years. Such as come within this description may apply by letter to B. D. at the York Coffee House, St James's Street, and the apparently most deserving will be enquired after. No kept Mistress or lady of Pleasure need apply.

Matrimonial Ads

The following matrimonial advertisements ran in American and English newspapers between 1775 and 1875.

MATRIMONIAL ADVERTISEMENT. I hereby give notice to all unmarried women that I, John Hobnail, am at this writing five and forty, a widower, and in want of a wife. As I wish no one to be mistaken, I have a good cottage with a couple of acres of land, for which I pay 2*l.* a-year. I have five children, four of them old enough to be in employment; three sides of bacon and some pigs ready for market. I should like to have a woman fit to take care of her house when I am out. I want no second family. She may be between 40 and 50 if she likes. A good sterling woman would be preferred, who would take care of the pigs.

OFFER OF MARRIAGE.

COUNT SARSFIELD, Lord Lucan, descendant of the royal branches of Lorraine and Capet, and other sovereigns of Europe, wishes to contract an alliance with a lady capable from her rank and talents of supporting the dignity and titles, which an alliance so honourable would confer on her. Address, Poste Restante à Paris.

TO GIRLS OF FORTUNE.—MATRIMONY.—A bachelor, young, amiable, handsome, of good family, and accustomed to move in the highest sphere of society, is embarrassed in his circumstances. Marriage is his only hope of extrication. This advertisement is inserted by one of his friends. Ingratitude was never one of his faults, and he will study for the remainder of his life to prove his estimation of the confidence placed in him. Address, post paid L. L. H. L., 47 King Street, Soho.—N.B. The witticisms of cockney scribblers deprecated.

A GENTLEMAN of position desires the society of a young lady or widow. Would afford moderate pecuniary aid to a respectable and deserving person. Address, with particulars, appointing interview, ——, Mercury office.

A STRANGER in New-York desires a few lady correspondents whom he can call upon, and who would be pleased to accompany him to theatres, &c. Address ——, New-York University.

A YOUNG MAN of refined taste would like to meet with a good-looking lady (not above twenty) who is engaged during the day. Address, appointing interview, ——, No. 4, Mercury office.

A LADY would like to meet with a gentleman who would thoroughly appreciate her exclusive society. For particulars, address ——, Box 2, No. 688 Broadway.

A GENTLEMAN, aged twenty-five, would be pleased to form the acquaintance of a young lady, or widow, under twenty-five years of age. Must be educated, and of good reputation. One engaged during the day preferred. A desirable party will meet with a permanent friend. Disreputable parties need not answer this. Address in confidence for ten days, —— ——, Mercury office.

A GENTLEMAN of means, alone in this city, desires the acquaintance of a respectable, genteel young lady of refinement, who is, like himself, friendless and alone; the most honorable secrecy observed. Address, with full particulars, ——, Mercury office, 128 Fulton-st., New-York.

A FRENCH GENTLEMAN, newly arrived in this country and lonely, wishes to form the acquaintance of a lady who could prove as true a friend to him as he would be to her. Address, in confidence, as discretion will be absolute, ——, Mercury office.

A YOUNG GENTLEMAN would like to make the acquaintance of an affectionate and sociable young lady who would appreciate a true friend; one residing in Brooklyn preferred. Address ——, box 3, 761 New-York P.O.

A GENTLEMAN OF MEANS wishes to make the acquaintance of a young lady of sixteen to eighteen years (blonde preferred); one who would appreciate a companion and friend may find one by addressing ——, Mercury office.

A YOUNG WIDOW would like to make the acquaintance of an elderly gentleman of means, who would be willing to assist her, in return for true friendship. No triflers need answer. Address ——, Station E.

TWO YOUNG MEN, residents of New-York, of some means, are desirous of forming the acquaintance of two ladies between the ages of sixteen and twenty-two, with a view to sociability and quiet enjoyment. To those that are worthy, pecuniary assistance will be willingly rendered, if necessary. Those employed in some light occupation preferred. Address, appointing interview, —— and ——, Mercury office.

⁂ I have undertaken to advertize all sorts of Things that are honourable, and what follows is not otherwise, and I am well paid for it:

☞ A Gentleman about 30 Years of Age, that says he has a Very Good Estate, would willingly Match Himself to some Young Gentlewoman that has a Fortune of £3000 or thereabout, And he will make Settlement to content.

When it shall appear that I am candid and no otherwise concerned than in bringing two Elderly Persons to a Treaty; and the nine Days Wonder and Laughter (usually attending new Things) are over, and that Nobody shall know Anything of the Matter, but where I shall reasonably believe they are in good earnest; then 'tis probable such Advertisements may prove very useful.

A Young Man about 25 Years of Age, in a very good Trade, and whose Father will make him worth £1000, would willingly embrace a suitable Match. He has been brought up a Dissenter with his Parents, and is a sober Man.

L. S. W., twenty-one, dark, and considered handsome, lithe in figure, of the medium height, and of a good family, would like to receive the carte-de-visite of a young lady, a blond preferred. He is shortly going abroad, probably to Mexico, or some of the republics adjacent, where he intends to make a name and fortune. He is very ambitious, and intends joining an army where there is active service. He wants a wife who would encourage his plans and undertakings. One who would share with him the toils of a camp life, or who would rule in Courts. One who would receive homage from the savage tribes of Northern and Central America, or would maintain her husband's position as an officer and gentleman of honour both at home and at Court. He is of a very loving disposition, though rather hasty, and to a lady who would do as he wished he would be an affectionate, loving husband, companion, and protector.

Ladies.

1st Class. I am twenty years of age, heiress to an estate in the county of Essex of the value of 30,000*l.*, well educated, and of domestic habits; of an agreeable, lively disposition, and genteel figure. Religion that of my future husband.

2nd Class. I am thirty years of age, a widow, in the grocery line in London—have children; of middle stature, full made, fair complexion and hair, temper agreeable, worth 3,000*l.*

3rd Class. I am tall and thin, a little lame in the hip, of a lively disposition, conversible, twenty years of age, live with my father, who, if I marry with his consent, will give me 1,000*l.*

4tn Class. I am twenty years of age; mild disposition and manners; allowed to be personable.

5th Class. I am sixty years of age; income limited; active, and rather agreeable.

Gentlemen.

1st Class. A young gentleman with dark eyes and hair; stout made; well educated; have an estate of 500*l.* per annum in the county of Kent; besides 10,000*l.* in three per cent. consolidated annuities; am of an affable disposition, and very affectionate.

2nd Class. I am forty years of age, tall and slender, fair complexion and hair, well tempered and of sober habits, have a situation in the Excise, of 300*l.* per annum, and a small estate in Wales of the annual value of 150*l.*

3rd Class. A tradesman in the city of Bristol, in a ready-money business, turning 150*l.* per week at a profit of 10 per cent., pretty well tempered, lively, and fond of home.

4th Class. I am fifty-eight years of age; a widower, without encumbrance; retired from business upon a small income; healthy constitution; and of domestic habits.

5th Class. I am twenty-five years of age; a mechanic of sober habits; industrious, and of respectable connections.

It is presumed that the public will not find any difficulty in describing themselves; if they should, they will have the assistance of the managers, who will be in attendance at the office, No. 5, Great St. Helens, Bishopsgate Street, on Mondays, Wednesdays, and Fridays, between the hours of eleven and three o'clock.—Please to inquire for Mr Jameson, up one pair of stairs. All letters to be post paid.

The subscribers are to be furnished with a list of descriptions, and when one occurs likely to suit, the parties may correspond; and if mutually approved, the interview may be afterwards arranged.

9971 VEGETARIAN, a young man who does not use flesh as food; a Roman Catholic, humble, well-educated, and connected. A lover of temperance, truth, literature, fruit, flowers, and economy, income about £80 a year, wishes for a wife with similar tastes, principles, and income, or as nearly so as possible.—The address with Editor.

AGENORIA says that she has natural golden-brown hair, fair oval face, laughing mischievous eyes, dark arched eyebrows, roguish expression of countenance, is eighteen, ladylike, sensible, merry, good-natured, highly respectable, and has good expectations. She longs to be married to a tall, studious, benevolent, affectionate, well-principled gentleman, who would think it a pleasure to instruct and assist her endeavours to obtain a thorough knowledge of English, French, and drawing; and in return she would try to be an apt pupil, and a loving and obedient wife.

MATRIMONY.

WANTED, by a young Gentleman just beginning House-keeping, a Lady, between eighteen and twenty-five Years of Age, with a good Education, and a Fortune not less than 5,000*l.*; sound Wind and Limb, Five Feet Four Inches without her Shoes; not fat, nor yet too lean; a clear Skin; sweet Breath, with good Set of Teeth; no Pride, nor Affectation; not very talkative, nor one that is deemed no Scold; but of a Spirit to resent an Affront; of a charitable Disposition; not over fond of Dress, though always decent and clean; that will entertain her Husband's Friends with Affability and Cheerfulness, and prefer his Company to public Diversions and gadding about; one who can keep his Secrets, that he may open his Heart to her without reserve on all Occasions; that can extend domestic Expenses with Economy, as Prosperity advances, without Ostentation; and retrench them with Cheerfulness, if Occasion should require.

Any Lady disposed to Matrimony, answering this Description, is desired to direct for Y. Z. at the Baptist's Head Coffee-House, Aldermanbury.

N.B. None but Principals will be treated with, nor need any apply that are deficient in any one Particular: the Gentleman can make adequate Return, and is, in every Respect, deserving a Lady with the above Qualifications.

TO GENTLEMEN OF FORTUNE.

A MOST advantageous Opportunity now offers to any young Gentleman of Character and independent Fortune; the Advertiser of this will introduce such to a most accomplished young Lady of Fortune, and greater Expectancy. None but a real Gentleman will succeed: therefore it is desired no other would apply. Letters directed to P. L. at the Nottingham Coffee-house, opposite Great Turnstile, Holborn, mentioning their present Condition, and where to inquire of the specified Particulars, signed with their own Name, will have due Regard and Honour, and Secrecy observed as it is required.

BRIDEWAIN.

There let Hymen oft appear
In saffron robe and taper clear,
And pomp and feast and revelry,
With mask and antic pageantry;
Such sights as youthful poets dream,
On summer eves by haunted stream.

GEORGE HAYTON, who married ANNE, the daughter of Joseph and Dinah Colin, of Crosby Mill, purposes having a BRIDEWAIN at his house, at Crosby near Maryport, on Thursday the 7th day of May next, where he will be happy to see his friends and well-wishers, for whose amusement there will be a variety of races, wrestling matches, etc. etc. The prizes will be—a saddle, two bridles, a pair of *gands d'amour* gloves, which whoever wins is sure to be married within the twelvemonth; a girdle (*ceinture de Venus*) possessing qualities not to be described; and many other articles, sports and pastimes too numerous to mention, but which can never prove tedious in the exhibition.

From fashion's laws and customs free,
We follow sweet variety;
By turns we laugh and dance and sing;
Time's for ever on the wing;
And nymphs and swains of Cumbria's plain
Present the golden age again.

195 A BACHELOR, 32, height 6 feet, strong, fair and considered good looking, closely connected with nobility, and moving in the best county society, one brother inherits entailed estates and two in the army, a member of one of the most particular west-end clubs, residence family mansion beautifully situated on the bank of a large river, disposition amiable and energetic, would not mind getting married, if I could meet a suitable wife. She must be of a loveable disposition, good figure and pleasing face, and have a fortune of not less than £10,000 to enable me to buy out the other partner in a large manufactory which cost £23,000, and yealds over £3,000 per annum, without which I will not become a benedict for years. Would like communicate with 9920, 9852, or 9803. Address L. M. A., Editor M. N., 282, Strand.

A GENTLEMAN of Fortune, whom Family reasons oblige to drop a connection which has for some time subsisted between him and an agreeable young Lady, will give a considerable sum of Money with her to any Gentleman, or person in genteel Business, who has good sense and resolution to despise the censures of the World, and will enter with her into the Holy state of Matrimony. Letters addressed to Mr G. H., at the Cecil Street Coffee-House, will be paid due attention to.

THE MARRIAGE BROKER

Accommodates Ladies and Gentlemen with everything in the matrimonial way which their Hearts can wish for (Virtue and Money only excepted), and that at first sight of the Parties, having fitted up a variety of very commodious Apartments.——He deals either in the ton or City Stile. If a difficult case, apply to our Attorney General, who attends me here in Person. N.B. I only charge five Guineas poundage per couple.

MARRIAGE TREATIES.

Ye Nymphs forlorn, who pine away in Shades!
Ye mournful Widows, wailing for—Brocades!
Coxcombs who sigh for—Mode! and sighing Wits!
Bucks of St. James's! and ye Half-moon'd Cits!
Ye old and young—the ugly and the fair!
To Hymen's Shrine haste, sacrifice despair.
Let Law divorce, tyrannic Husbands rail,
Hence dare their Ire!—for here's enough for sale.
Let Virtue's mask the Wife awhile pursue,
Here's fresh Supply—here Wives of ev'ry Hue!
Black, white, red, grey—the bright, the dull, the witty!
Here's Dames for Courtiers, misses for the City!

COUNT SARSFIELD LUCAN, lineal descendant of the royal line of Lorraine and Capet, and other sovereigns of Europe, desires to join in an alliance of marriage with a lady whose qualities and abilities will enable her to support the rank and titles she will obtain by this honourable alliance. Address to Count Sarsfield Lucan, Poste Restante à Paris.

"Oh, woman, in our hours of ease,
Uncertain, coy, and hard to please;
When pain or sickness rend the brow,
A ministering angel thou."

9828 A Young WIDOW, highly connected, dark hair and eyes, considered pretty, good income, desires to marry, she does not deny that she might at times realize the two first lines of the couplet quoted above, but she can assure any gentleman willing to make the experiment that she is as certain to be true to the conclusion. Address with Editor.

Married, yesterday at S. James's church by the right rev. Dr Hen. Egerton, lord bishop of Hereford, the hon. Francis Godolphin, of Scotland-yard, Esq; to the 3d daughter of the countess of Portland, a beautiful lady of 50,000l. fortune. *P.*——Will. Godolphin, Esq; to the lady Barbara Bentinck, &c. *D.P.*——At the chapel-royal, at S. James's: youngest daughter, &c. *D, J. D. A.*

Married a few days since —— Price, a Buckinghamshire gentleman of near 2000l. per ann. to miss Robinson of the Theatre Royal in Drury-lane. *L. E.*——On tuesday, the lord Visc. Faulkland to the lady Villew, relict of the late lord Faukland, a lady of great merit and fortune. *D. P.*——Mr Price's marriage is entirely false and groundless. *D. A. Ap.* 24.

Miscellaneous Madness

The following American handbills and advertisements were originally produced between 1840 and 1890.

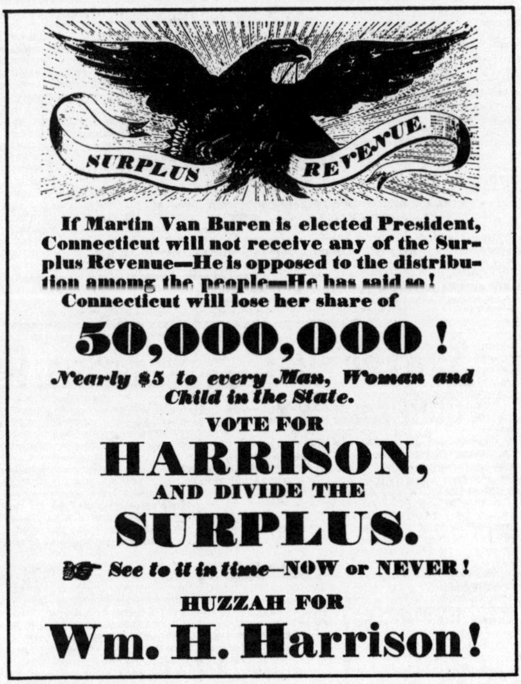

Fourth Book No. 4.

OF THE

FRANKLIN SQUARE SONG COLLECTION.

Now Ready. Uniform in Size, Style, and Character of Contents with **Nos. 1, 2 and 3.** Many Old Tunes. It **contains 200 Favorite Songs and Hymns** with music arranged in Four Parts, among which are the following: Angel of Peace—Are There Tidings?—Autumn Dreaming—Awake, My Soul—Battle Eve—Bring Flowers—Brookside—Canadian Boat Song—Clang of the Wooden Shoon—Come, Holy Spirit—Come to the Sea—Come Unto Him—Darby and Joan—Dear Little Shamrock—Dermot Astore—Distant Drum—Dublin Bay—Ehren on the Rhine—Ever be Happy—Exile of Erin—Fallen is Thy Throne—Fire of Home—Flowers for the Brave—Forever and Forever—Forsaken Am I—Gently Rest—Golden Days—Go to Sleep, Lena Darling—Greenwood Tree—Happy Are We—Hearts of Oak—Heaven is My Home—Heavily Wears the Day—I Come, I Come!—I'm a Pilgrim—Innisfail—In the Gloaming—I Would I Were a Boy Again—Keller's American Hymn—Kerry Dance—Let Me Dream Again—Low-Backed Car—Lucy's Flittin'—Lurlaline—May Margaret—My Nannie's Awa'—Nursery Songs—Oh, Wert Thou in the Cauld Blast?—Old Tubal Cain—Old Oaken Bucket—One by One the Sands are Flowing—Ossian's Serenade—Play-Time Songs—Poor Tho' My Cot—Punchinello—Rataplan—Rock Me to Sleep, Mother—Soldiers' Chorus—Strangers Yet—Sweeter than the Breath of Morning—The Night is Fine—The Old Sexton—The Pilot—The Sound of Harps—Thoughts of Wonder—Thou'rt Like Unto a Flower—Thou Wilt Never Grow Old—Three Fishers—Trancadillo—Twilight Dews—Vesper Chimes—What Are the Wild Waves Saying?—When I Remember—Who Shall Be Fairest? Etc. Together with 125 others not here named, and much appropriate Reading Matter. No leaf turned to complete any song or hymn. Elements of Music, Eight Pages, One Hundred Points. Send Postal Card for Contents of the Four Numbers.

Good books for Home or School. **Two Hundred** Songs and Hymns, upon **184** Pages, in each book. Same Size and Shape as Harper's Monthly Magazine. **Paper, 50 cts.; Boards, 60 cts.; Cloth, $1.00.** Address,

Harper & Brothers, New York.

PROTECTION CUSPADORES.

Secured to heavy 12 in. Mat, cannot tip over. Saves carpet and floor. Made of tin, brass and china. Useful, durable and ornamental.

Expressed, prepaid, to any part of the United States, east of Denver, upon receipt of cash as follows:

No. 1, Tin, handsomely ornamented.....	**$ 75**	**each.**
" 2, do. with Umbrella Rests....	**1 00**	**"**
" 3, Nickel-Plated on Tin.........	**1 50**	**"**
" 4, do. with Umbrella Rests....	**2 00**	**"**
" 5, Terra Cotta, ornamented..........	**1 75**	**"**
" 7, China.......	**2 25**	**"**
" 8, Nickel on Brass, decorated mats...	**2 25**	**"**
" 9, " " nickel-plated mats,	**2 50**	**"**

For sale to the trade in quantities.

THE ADAMS & WESTLAKE MFG. CO.

Chicago. Boston. New York.

These two gentlemen are brothers. One uses SO ZODONT, the other does not. The former has ha his moustache shaved off, and always laughs; th latter wears his very long, and never laughs.

PERSONS AFRAID TO LAUGH

For fear of showing a neglected set of teetl should cleanse them night and morning with th aromatic invigorating

SOZODONT

If the teeth begin to show signs of decay, us SOZODONT at once and often. Rely upon it, an they will be rescued from impending ruin. Th formula of this preparation includes only botani ingredients, and contains only the purest and mos salutary of these. Use no other dentifrice bu SOZODONT. It is pure, effective, and fragran

Sold by Druggists and Fancy-goods Dealers.

A BEAUTIFUL HOUSE FOR $1200

* * * **This marvelous house has been built more than 300 times from our plans;** *it is so well planned* **that it affords ample room even for a large family. 1st floor shown above; on 2d floor are 4 bed rooms and in attic 2 more. Plenty of Closets. The whole warmed by one chimney.**

Large illustrations and full description of the above as well as of 39 other houses, ranging in cost from $400 up to $6,500, may be found in "SHOPPELL'S MODERN LOW-COST HOUSES," a large quarto pamphlet, showing also how to select sites, get loans, &c. Sent postpaid on receipt of 50c. Stamps taken, or send $1 bill and we will return the change. Address, BUILDING PLAN ASSOCIATION, (Mention this Paper.) 24 Beekman St., (Box 2702,) N. Y.

TALLEYRAND, *the French Statesman, and friend of the great Napoleon, being asked if Napoleon shaved himself, replied: "Oh, yes! They who are born to kingdoms have some one to shave them, BUT THEY WHO ACQUIRE KINGDOMS, SHAVE THEMSELVES.*

PETER THE GREAT, *with his determined passion for reform, proclaimed a tax upon beards, and finally decreed that any subject who continued to wear one should have it removed with pincers, or be shaven with a blunt razor.*

Thus the resolute monarch succeeded in smoothing the face of nearly every subject in his kingdom, and the practice of shaving became almost universal in Europe.

Gentlemen who Shave Themselves will derive Ease, Comfort, and Pleasure from the use of

WILLIAMS' SHAVING STICK.

This EXQUISITE TOILET ARTICLE contains all of those rich and lasting qualities which have made our "GENUINE YANKEE SHAVING SOAP" famous for 50 years. Delicately scented with finely selected Attar of Roses. Each Stick in a neat Wood Case covered with Red Morocco Leatherette. Very Portable. Indispensable to Travellers. A Convenience and Luxury for all who Shave.

If your Druggist does not keep Williams' Shaving Soaps they will be sent, postpaid, to any address upon receipt of price in stamps or currency, as follows: WILLIAMS' SHAVING STICK, **25** cts. GENUINE YANKEE SOAP, **15** cts. WILLIAMS' CELEBRATED BARBERS' SOAP—FOR TOILET USE. Remarkable for Purity. Mild and Healing Qualities. Endorsed by Eminent Physicians. Unequalled for Allaying the Roughness and Irritation of the Skin commonly suffered by Infants and Young Children.

THE ADIRONDACK RAILWAY.

ACROSS THE DIVIDE.

Saratoga to North Creek, The Upper Hudson, Adirondack Mountains, Lakes, and Rivers.

THE

DIRECT ROUTE

—FOR—

Lakes **Luzerne, Schroon, Blue Mountain, Raquette, Tupper's, Long, Jessup's Landing, Buttermilk Falls,** and all the most picturesque resorts in the

GREAT ADIRONDACK WILDERNESS.

FROM NEW YORK. A Special through Wagner Sleeper will leave Grand Central Depot every week day during the season at 6.30 P.M. Arrive North Creek 6.30 A.M.; Blue Mountain Lake, by stage, 1.35 P.M., and Raquette Lake by steamer, 6 P.M., same day.

☞ Send 6 cents in stamps to The Adirondack Railway Company, 45 Broadway, New York; or Saratoga Springs, for new edition of "Birch Bark," an Illustrated Guide, with colored maps, time tables, and full information.

THE ADIRONDACK RY

W. W. DURANT, Gen'l Manager.
C. E. DURKEE, Sup't.

Pears'
Soap
PEARS'
SOAP
YOU DIRTY BOY
You Dirty Boy!
The best for the Complexion. A "balm for the Skin."
The most economical; it wears to thinness of a wafer.

TO ARMS!

CITIZENS OF HEMPSTEAD AND NORTH HEMPSTEAD,

DO YOU HEAR THE CALL OF YOUR COUNTRY, BECKONING YOU TO ARMS?

BY THE FOLLOWING ORDER--

"Special Orders, to wit (12): CAPT WILLIS, 119th Reg't N. Y. V., is detailed on the Recruiting service, and will report for instructions to the Superintendent of the Recruiting Service of the State of New York.

By Command of MAJOR-GENERAL McCLELLAN,
RICH'D B. IRWIN, CAPT., A. D. C., A. A. A. G."...

I am with you again, but a few days only! I want to take back with me to Washington 100 MEN! They must be had in six days! The hour is at hand! Fellow-Citizens, will you Respond? Your proud past speaks for you.

Show your Countrymen that you choose Honor and Glory before humiliation and shame. Let every man attend a

Grand Mass Meeting

TO BE HELD AT HEMPSTEAD,

WEDNESDAY, SEPT. 17, '62,

AT HEWLETT'S HOTEL,

AT HALF-PAST SEVEN O'CLOCK P. M.

☞ **Citizens, prove yourselves worthy of the 19th Century.**

BENJ. A. WILLIS,
Capt. Co. H, 119th Reg't N. Y. V.

BAKER & GODWIN, Printers, Printing-House Square, opposite City Hall, N. Y

HOMES.

Jere. Johnson, Jr., is selling superb Lots in the 26th ward of Brooklyn, at Bath Beach Junction, and at Woodside Heights for $100 and upward, payable $5 and $10 monthly; free excursions daily to Bath Beach Junction and Woodside Heights. For maps and tickets, apply at the offices of **JERE. JOHNSON, Jr., 60 Liberty St., New York, and 393 Fulton St., Brooklyn.**

SAVE MONEY

By Ordering
FASHIONABLE CUSTOM CLOTHING
from
New York.

ELEGANT SUITS
TO ORDER.
$18, $20, and $25.
DRESS SUITS,
$20 to $35.
TROUSERS,
$5 to $8.

WE SEND FREE
Samples of Cloths and Suitings and Fashion Plates, with full directions for ordering Gents' Clothing and Furnishing Goods, by mail, with fit and satisfaction guaranteed. Send for samples. Mention color and price desired, and give trial order to

GEO. W. LOSS & SON
(Established 1852),
Fashionable Clothiers,
70 & 72 Fulton St., N. Y.

CAUTION!—Some dealers recommend inferior goods in order to make a larger profit. This is the **original** $3 Shoe. Beware of imitations which acknowledge their own inferiority by attempting to build upon the reputation of the original. **You cannot** be sure of getting the **genuine** article unless you are careful to examine and see that this stamp appears plainly on the soles:

JAMES MEANS' $3 SHOE.

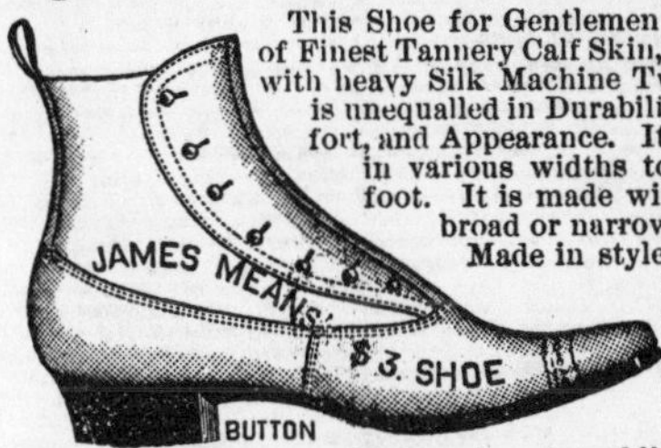

This Shoe for Gentlemen is made of Finest Tannery Calf Skin, stitched with heavy Silk Machine Twist, and is unequalled in Durability, Comfort, and Appearance. It is made in various widths to fit any foot. It is made with either broad or narrow toes. Made in styles shown in cut, also in Congress or Lace. The quality of this Shoe has won for it so high a place in public estimation that it stands to-day absolutely without a rival. Wherever you live, this Shoe is within your reach. Ask your dealer for it, and if he cannot supply you with a good fit, send your address on postal card to
JAMES MEANS & CO., 42 Lincoln St., Boston, Mass.

Just too Funny For Anything! **"SAMANTHA AT SARATOGA"**
BRIGHT HITS. COMIC CUTS. SELLS LIKE FUN.

SOLD ONLY BY SUBSCRIPTION.

And it wuz anon that we see in the distance a fair, white female a standin' kinder still in the edge of the woods, and Josiah spoke in a seemingly careless way, and sez he:

"She don't seem to have many clothes on, Samantha."

Sez I, "Hush! Josiah, she has probable overslept herself, and come out in a hurry, mebby to look for some herbs or sunthin, I persume one of her children are sick, and she sprung right up out of bed, and come out to get some mother wort, or catnip or sunthin."—

And as I spoke I drawed Josiah down a side path away from her.

But he stopped stun still, and sez he, "Mebby I ort to go and help her, Samantha."

Sez I, "Josiah Allen, sense I've lived with you, I don't think I have been *shameder* of you—sez I. It would mortify her to death if she should *mistrust* you had seen her in that condition."

"Wall," sez he, still a hangin' back, "if the child is *very* sick, and I can be any help to her, it is my *duty* to go."

His eye had been on her nearly every moment of the time, in spite of my almost voyalent protests, and sez he kinder excited like—"She is standin' stun still, as if she is skairt, mebby there is a snake in front of her, or sunthin, or mebby she is took paralyzed, I'd better go and see."

Sez I, in low, deep axents, "you stay right where you be, Josiah Allen, and I will go forward, and if we need your help, I will holler." And finally he consented after a parley.

"*Wall, as I got up to her I see she wuznt a live meat woman, but a statute.*"

Written amid the *whirl of fashion* at **Saratoga**, it takes off its **follies, flirtations,** low neck dressing, **dudes, pug dogs,** the **water craze, tobogganing,** etc., in the author's inimitable *mirth-provoking* style. The (100) illustrations by "Opper" are **"just killing."** People crazy to get it. **Selling like Hot Cakes.**
Price $2.50. AGENTS WANTED. Apply to **HUBBARD BROS., Pubs., PHILADELPHIA, PA.**

KAHNWEILER'S
IMPROVED PATENT
CORK LIFE-PRESERVER,

For Swimming and Boating. Is easily adjusted. Any person can learn to swim in a very short time. Can be worn under the bathing-suit without being noticed. Assorted sizes for Ladies and Children. Price $1.50; any size mailed or expressed on receipt of $2.00.

D. KAHNWEILER,
146 Worth St., N. Y.

The Favorite.

A grand gift. Pleases everybody. A model of luxury and convenience, in sickness or in health. 50 changes of position. Simple, elegant, durable. Unlike other chairs, it can be adjusted by the one sitting in it. We also manufacture Wheel and Physicians' Chairs. Catalogue free. Mention this paper.

Stevens Chair Co.,
No. 3 Sixth St.,
Pittsburg, Pa.

THE
Claudent.

BEST SCARF

EVER MADE.

This novel Scarf **FOR GENTLEMEN** derives its name from the Latin word "Claudens," to draw together. Owing to the ingenious construction of the shield, when adjusted to the wearer, the round corners draw inwards, conforming in its graceful outlines to the neck and chest. Examine carefully for the **Patent Stamp** on the back of each Scarf. None others are genuine. For sale at all first-class establishments.

FISK, CLARK & FLAGG, Patentees.

FLORIDA LOTS $15

40X100 feet.

Lots **40x100 ft. in Silver Springs Park, Florida,** only $15. High, dry land. No swamps or malaria. Over 2 600 merchants and professional people of every kind, also ladies, have already invested; new arrivals weekly; 88 Houses, 2 Hotels, 1 Church, 1 School House and 8 Stores, built last 10 months Six Daily Trains. Every man, woman and child should own a lot in the land of oranges, lemons, bananas. pine apples, sunshine, tropical scenery and health. **A shrewd and popular investment.** Prices will soon be doubled. 5-Acre Orange Grove Tracts, $250. Free R. R. Ticket to Florida. REFERENCE.—Wm. H. Oakley, Prest. Nat. Citizens Bank, N. Y. A 16-page descriptive paper, 24 engravings showing cottages, also plat of town showing avenues, &c., *sent free.* Address, **L. N. MOWRY,** President, **No. 179 BROADWAY, NEW YORK,** or **SILVER SPRINGS PARK, MARION CO., FLORIDA.**

For the Toilet.

Ayer's Hair Vigor is indispensable to a complete toilet. It is an agreeably perfumed dressing, and renders the hair soft and lustrous. It stimulates weak and thin hair to renewed growth, and restores faded or gray hair to its original color and beauty.

"I have used Ayer's Hair Vigor for a number of years, and it has always given me satisfaction. It is an excellent dressing, prevents the hair from turning gray, insures its vigorous growth, and keeps the scalp white and clean."

MARY A. JACKSON,
Salem, Mass.

"I had been gray for nearly ten years before commencing the use of

Ayer's Hair Vigor.

Since using it my hair has been restored to its original color, and very much increased in growth."

ETHEL TROTTER, Norfolk, Va.

"Several years ago I was afflicted with a humor in my scalp, which caused my hair to fall out, so that I became nearly bald. The use of Ayer's Hair Vigor cured me of the humor, checked the falling out of hair, and restored it to its original healthy condition."

J. B. YOUNG, Carrollton, Md.

Ayer's Hair Vigor,

PREPARED BY
DR. J. C. AYER & CO., Lowell, Mass.
Sold by all Druggists.